My Parents Got a Divorce

compiled by Gary Sprague

D0048432

Chariot Books
David C. Cook Publishing Co.

Chariot Books™ is an imprint of David C. Cook Publishing Co.
David C. Cook Publishing Co., Elgin, Illinois 60120
David C. Cook Publishing Co., Weston, Ontario
Nova Distribution Ltd., Newton Abbot, England

MY PARENTS GOT A DIVORCE
Designed and illustrated by Michael Boze
First Printing, 1992
Printed in the United States of America
96 95 94 93   5 4 3 2

Library of Congress Cataloging-in-Publication Data

My parents got a divorce: Christian kids tell how they went from
hurt to hope / [edited by] Gary A. Sprague.
      p.   cm.
      Summary: Christian students discuss how they learned to
deal with their parents' breakup.
      ISBN 0-7814-0486-X
      1. Children of divorced parents—United States—Juvenile
literature. 2. Divorce—Religious aspects—Christianity—
Juvenile literature. [1. Divorce. 2. Christian life.] I. Sprague,
Gary A.
HQ777.5.M9 1992
306.89—dc20
            91-43023

                  CIP

                  AC

To Justin

for the courage to continue loving both of your parents, even in the midst of the pain. You have proven that God is faithful and can do great things in our lives.

Table of Contents

Foreword

I was once a host for one of those early morning television talk shows. I interviewed all kinds of people about all kinds of things in an effort to make for some interesting broadcast time.

One morning I was interviewing a couple who had written a book on "creative divorce." They spent most of our hour together trying to convince me and the TV audience that they had found the secret to dissolving a marriage without acrimony or rancor.

It was all so lighthearted and fluffy. They giggled and joked and tried very hard to make the point that they were really better friends now that they were divorced than they had ever been before.

They explained how their marriage had stifled their creativity and individuality. They made rambling speeches sprinkled with the phrases that we all have learned to expect from those who are "high" on the Human Potential Movement. In the course of the interview they explained how the divorce had freed each of them up "to find their true selves" and "to actualize their respective personhoods." They talked about the ways that they "realized who they really were through the painful process of self-definition that goes on during the struggles of divorce." It was the kind of chatter that fills an hour of broadcast time and leaves the viewer wondering why he or she bothered to watch.

I was not the least bit judgmental until the last few minutes of the show. *After all*, I thought to myself, *if that's what they want to do, it's a free country.*

My easygoing acceptance of these guests who seemed to deal with marriage and divorce in such a cavalier manner quickly ended when they happened to mention their children. When I found out that children had been caught in the mess, I could not help but seriously zero in on them and ask, as pointedly as I knew how, "How does all of this affect your kids?"

The two of them tried to explain that, while it was difficult at first, the children had learned to accept the divorce and were now "perfectly adjusted." The woman talked of all the "love" that her children were receiving at their day-care center. She smiled and said that it was undoubtedly more healthy for them to be spending eight hours each day with "professionals" who know how to raise children than to be "stuck" with their mother all day.

Dad tried to convince me that although he only saw the children every other weekend, he had a close and healthy relationship with them.

There was no need for me to strip bare their arguments and declarations. The phoniness of it all was too obvious to deserve comment. I just let them go on and on making their claims that "if handled properly divorce has no adverse effects on children."

When the show ended, one of the cameramen muttered to me under his breath, "Who do they think they are kidding besides themselves?"

Divorce is a disaster! Let none of those glib, pop psychologists like Dr. Ruth claim that it can be otherwise. The research is piling in. Divorce is so disruptive in the lives of children that it is cited as a major factor leading to drug use, premarital sex, and delinquency.

This is not to say that such results necessarily flow from a divorce. It is only to point out that such behavioral patterns are more likely to be evident among children of divorced couples than among children from intact families. Research indicates that the only thing that is worse than divorce is desertion. In the latter case the pain and guilt often prove too much for children to bear.

There are a wide range of painful reactions to divorce. Some children blame themselves for what has happened, thinking that if they had been better children, Daddy would not have left.

Others are consumed with seething anger and spend their lives working out their aggression on innocent people who just happen to be available.

But what is saddest of all is that among the children of the divorced there is a strong likelihood that they will repeat the same mistakes their parents made. The children of divorced couples are much more likely than the children from intact families to experience marital disruption and to have severe problems in relating to the opposite sex. Indeed there is ample evidence to support the biblical declaration, "The sins of the fathers shall be upon the children and the children's children." Divorce has far-reaching consequences.

The eruption of the divorce epidemic in the life of the church is a relatively new phenomenon, and the church is ill-prepared to handle it. It is even less prepared to deal with the consequences of divorce in the lives of the children who are directly involved. We must take note of the fact that just fifty years ago divorce was a rarity in the life of the church, and most pastors were reluctant, if not downright opposed, to remarrying those who had been through divorce.

Everything is changed today. Divorce impacts every congregation, and the problem even has become common among the clergy. It is not just the "liberal" churches that have come to accept divorce with little complaint, but old-fashioned fundamentalist churches have gotten used to divorce, too.

Generally church people try not to notice divorces. They practice a kind of collective repression and go on about their ecclesiastical business as though nothing really has happened. They accept the new wives and husbands, and seldom ask what might be embarrassing questions about what happened to the old ones. And the children of divorce are treated as though nothing traumatic has happened in their lives.

Well, something traumatic has happened. And this book will give you keen insights as to just what the victims of divorce go through. With letters and interviews gathered from children he has counseled, Gary Sprague enables us to enter into the subjective consciousness of children who suffer because their parents are no longer together.

The children's descriptions and explanations are meant to help others who are going through divorce or who have been through divorce. They share their experiences so that all of us can better understand what children are experiencing and how we can better participate in the healing process.

Out of his own ministry to the children of divorced parents, Gary tries to help those who must endure divorce (try as they may to make their marriages work). But how can they soothe the agony of their children? Gary tries to make it clear that no matter how painful the end of a marriage may be for the children of the divorced, "there is a balm in Gilead" that can heal and restore the brokenhearted.

Divorced parents cannot afford to ignore the pain of their children, and this book may help them pay attention to that pain in a redemptive and healing fashion.

Tony Campolo
Professor of Sociology
Eastern College, St. Davids, Pa.

Introduction

You're not alone.

That can be a really comforting thought. So often, when your parents divorce, you feel like you're alone. You feel somehow that it's your fault. You feel that nobody could possibly understand all the crazy feelings twisting around inside of you.

The best thing that someone can say to you is, "Hey, I've been there. You're not alone." That's what this book is all about. All of the kids in this book are real kids just like you. They've all been through the experience of having parents separate or divorce. They're sharing their feelings of what it was like for them in order for you to know that other kids are feeling the same things that you are feeling. Hopefully this will make you feel better.

We have an organization called Fresh Start Seminars. It began as a way to help people deal with their own divorces. But soon we realized that there were a lot of kids who needed help dealing with their parents' divorces. So we started some meetings for children of divorce called Fresh Start for Kids.

These have been amazing meetings. I recently spoke with a young woman who had gone to one of these meetings as a teenager. "Many times I didn't even know how I felt," she said. "I knew I was confused. Then I would hear the other students talk about their anger toward their mom or dad, and it would suddenly 'click' with me that I felt the same way."

She says that she is "over" the divorce now. Talking and listening to others helped her deal with the feelings she had. But, she adds, "I've met many kids in school who are still carrying around a lot of anger because they've never gotten in touch with some of those same emotions we discussed in our group."

I wish that all the readers of this book could come to a Fresh Start for Kids Seminar. Maybe some of you have (or will). But this book is a way of taking some of the good things from those meetings and putting them in a package. We hope you can unwrap this package and find the help that you need.

You will read stories from students of different ages and backgrounds. We hope that you'll be able to identify with a few of these. We're really proud of these writers who took the time—and the courage—to write out their experiences.

Goals of This Book

1) We want it to help you become aware of your own feelings. "Oh, yeah? I've felt like that!"

2) We want you to remember that you are not alone in your feelings. There's no question about it—you're going through some tough stuff. But your feelings are probably pretty normal. Others have gotten through this, and you can, too.

3) We want you to see how these people have grown. You will be following the lives of the same students from chapter to chapter. You will see how they learned—step by step—to deal with their parents' breakup.

Yes, God can take a horrible mess and turn it into something good in your life. This will definitely take time, but I believe it can make us better people. I know, because I've seen it happen not only in my life, but also in the lives of hundreds of other young people and adults.

How to Use This Book

This book is divided into five chapters. Each chapter covers a different part of the divorce experience. Within each chapter are the stories of real students we have spoken with. We have listed their first names and their ages so that, if you like, you can pick out someone who is close to your own age and read his or her story. You can follow the same person through different chapters, or you can choose to read all of the stories.

Another way to read the book is to look at the chapter titles, and pick a chapter that discusses the kinds of things you are struggling with right now. Then turn to that chapter and read all of the students' comments.

Whatever way you choose to go through this book, it might be best to do it with someone else. That might be your mother or father. Even if it's been hard to talk to your parents lately, this might be a way to let them know how you're feeling. If your mom or dad isn't interested, then maybe a brother or sister might read it with you—or maybe a good friend whose parents have also divorced.

Always compare the feelings you're reading about with your own feelings. Don't "stuff" you feelings; let someone know about them. There are a lot of people out there—parents, brothers or sisters, friends, teachers, people at church—who really care about you. Some people think that the best way to work through your problems is on your own, by yourself. No way! At any age, smart people figure out where to go for help, and then they get it. They don't try to deal with their problems all by themselves.

We hope you enjoy reading this book and that it will help you feel better about being a kid whose parents got a divorce.

Note to Parents

This book has grown out of a divorce recovery program called Fresh Start Seminars. This program ministers to the separated and divorced throughout the country via radio, seminars, and publications. Fresh Start's program designed for children of divorce is called Kids in the Middle Seminars. We'd be happy to send you information about any of our programs or publications.

Fresh Start Seminars, Inc.
Fresh Start for Kids
63 Chestnut Road
Paoli, Pennsylvania 19301
1-800-882-2799

Chapter 1

How I Felt

It sort of makes you feel like you don't want them to, but sometimes it's for the better so they don't fight anymore. I didn't want them to separate. When my dad told me, we were at the dinner table. I cried because I was sad and then I hugged my dad. I was mad and I told him that I didn't want him to leave. I wanted them to stay together. I wasn't really mad at any one specific person because it wasn't really anyone's fault. I was just mad that they had to split up. I started feeling better when I went over to my dad's new apartment and saw where he was going to be living. That helped a lot.

Travis age 13

I was not happy. I was sad and I cried a lot. My dad told me when we were in the car, and he said he was going to move out because he and my mother were not getting along very well. Sometimes I was glad because I didn't have to listen to them fight anymore. I thought it would be good for them for a while. I was angry at both of my parents when they were yelling a lot. Sometimes my dad left the house after he had a fight with my mom. I was scared that he would not come back. I can talk to my friends and

Lauren age 10

my teacher if I am sad about something, but I try not to think about it anymore.

It feels sad because you miss the person who left, and you don't know if you will ever see him again. I was just a baby when my dad left, and I didn't see him until I was five years old. I don't know if or when I will see him again and that makes me sad.

Karla age 7

Well, it feels sort of sad because you don't expect it to happen. It catches you off guard. It takes you by surprise. Sometimes when I see other kids playing with their dads, I miss my dad and wish that my parents never got divorced. Sometimes I get mad that they got divorced, but one day my dad came to visit me. It was fun to visit with him, but it was sad to see him leave.

Josh 9

It is surprising and shocking because you are not ready for it at all. It comes out of nowhere. It is like someone dying or having a heart attack. When my dad first told us, we all laughed because we didn't know what else to do. We were all uncomfortable. Then we all started to cry because the shock was over. I was sad off and on for about six months. When I went to school I would forget about it, but then when I came home I would remember that my parents were divorced and I would be sad again. My mom reassured me that the divorce was not my fault and that helped a lot. My dad told me why they were getting divorced and that was helpful to know.

Carrie age 15

It feels sad, but when I kept busy at school, I would forget about it. My dad told us that they were getting a divorce and that he had a girlfriend. I was sad, but I didn't really cry. My dad cried. He felt really bad about it. I was scared and wondered if I was ever going to see my dad again before they worked out the visitation arrangements.

Mandy
age 8

At first you feel really hurt inside. You are feeling sad and you don't know what to do about it. I knew something was wrong when I went camping with my daddy. We were in the car and he started crying all of a sudden. He told me that my mom wanted to get a divorce and didn't love him anymore. Later my mom sat us down and said that she didn't love our daddy anymore and that she was going to leave. My dad told us to go to our room. When we came back down we saw our mom leaving and she didn't even say good-bye to us. She slammed the door and drove away really fast. I was so angry at my mom after that. I tore up my bed and kicked the wall to get my anger out. It was better to let out my anger because if I kept it inside, I would get sick to my stomach, feel real bad, and not want to go to school. After crying for about two months I realized I didn't do anything to cause my parents to split up, so I didn't need to be worried about it. Some kids think that it was their fault that their parents got divorced, but I would say that it isn't their fault. Parents love their kids, and the reason they get divorced is there's a problem between the two of them and not with you. After a while you just get away from it all and start to feel better about it.

John
age 11

At first it was kind of hard for me. I felt rejected because I felt it was my fault. I later realized that my dad left for his own reasons and not because of anything that I had done. I also felt a little lonely. It hurt really bad. I was down, depressed, and sad a lot because I was without a dad. I had an empty feeling inside of me. Even though my dad had visitation rights, I chose not to see him. It has been more than two years since I have seen my dad. I was angry with my dad at first for what he had done. He had always said that he loved my mom, and I wondered if he was lying to her.

*Mandi
age 15*

It feels like a hurt that won't go away. I felt like my mom was pulling on one arm and my dad was pulling on the other arm. When they didn't get along they would both tell me things about the other parent, and I didn't know who to believe. There was a lot of sadness. I lived with my dad, and when I visited my mom on the weekend, it was hard when I was leaving to come back home.

*Kelly
age 11*

Part of the time I felt guilty and that my dad didn't like me. I felt like the divorce was partly my fault. I regret that it happened because I would like to have a dad, but I don't, so I just live with it. When my dad left, I didn't know what was going on, so it didn't bother me. I didn't realize that it was going to be a permanent thing and that my life would change as a result of the divorce. Knowing why my dad left helped me to realize that it wasn't my fault. I was angry at my dad and didn't always want to go visit him on the weekends. I'm afraid sometimes that my dad will hurt me because he is very tall, strong, and has a very bad

*Amanda
age 13*

temper. My stepmother doesn't yell at us, but she tells my dad to yell at us and I worry for my stepsister. My stepmom can hurt you verbally by putting you down. I also worry about finances and having enough money to do things.

Right when they told me, I cried because I felt really bad. Then after a while I just went on with my life.

Chris age 9

When my dad first moved out it kind of felt like I was losing half of my life. I was very sad because I didn't really understand what was happening. I remember being angry because I was confused.

Becky age 11

It hurts at first because you are used to everybody being together. I had a lot of guilt, and I thought that the divorce was my fault. Toward the end, my parents seemed to always get into fights about me. Later I realized, through the help of counselors, that the divorce wasn't my fault. After a while, my parents told me why they were getting divorced and that helped, too. I was angry at my dad because he was the one who caused the divorce. I went through a lot of depression, and I still go through it now because I don't get along very well with my dad. I used to visit him every other weekend, but every time I went I fought with my stepmother, so now I don't visit very often at all.

Anne age 16

I think it is harder when your parents divorce than if one of your parents has died. If your parent dies, you can start and end the grief recovery process in a shorter amount of time. When your parents divorce, the conflict keeps going on for years, and it is hard to actually grieve over the fact that they are divorced. Every day it is something new to adjust to, whether it is a fight or a new dating partner. The feelings that you get are sort of indescribable. I get angry one day with my dad and the next day I get angry with my mom. Sometimes I feel bad for my brother and sister. I get angry that my friends don't understand how I feel.

Toni
Age 14

My feelings have been up in the air for the past two and a half years. However, I've learned to understand that the anger and frustration will ease as time goes on. In a split home situation, it is very easy to get manipulated. You may be kind of forced to feel certain ways; however, be certain you've made your own judgments. Only then can you make your own opinions.

It is very confusing because you don't know what is going on. You don't ask any questions, and you leave a lot up to your imagination. You don't understand why your parents are always fighting. I put myself in the middle sometimes. If one parent was mad at me, I would run to the other. I would try to start arguments between them so that I would get what I wanted, but in the end I was the one who lost. I cried a lot and sometimes used the divorce as an excuse not to do my homework.

Jessica
Age 15

I was really confused and upset when my parents first told me they were getting a divorce. I didn't know why they were splitting up. I thought it was my fault until my dad told me the reason why. My parents just got sick of each other. I cried a lot. I thought that divorce was something that happened to other people and never thought that it would happen to me. I felt like my world was crumbling around me. When my dad first told me about it, my sister and I came up with an idea to send my mom some flowers and say that they were from my dad so that they would get back together again. I was angry also because I didn't know what was going to happen.

Lauren
age 13

It feels lonely and like nobody is really there. I was angry at my dad because he had custody of us and we couldn't live with my mom. I didn't like it and felt like it just wasn't right. I was sad and withdrew from life and didn't go out very much.

Jennifer
Age 17

I missed my dad a lot when he left. It feels kind of sad because one parent is gone and you can't do as much with him anymore. I couldn't talk to my friends about the divorce because none of their parents were divorced. I could talk to my family though.

David
age 9

I felt confused because I did not know what was happening, and I felt afraid because I thought I would never see my parents again and that my parents would not see each other again. I felt helpless because there was nothing I could do to get them together again, hopeless because there was no hope for them to get back together again, lonely

Zack
Age 9

because we had to keep moving to different houses and apartments, and I had to make new friends over and over again. I felt worried that something would happen to my mom or dad because they were lonely without each other, and that someone would break into the house and get them when I was not there, and if I was there I could run to get help.

When my mom and dad divorced, I felt like it was the end of the world. I ran to my bedroom and started to cry. At first I thought it was my fault, but my mom told me it was not my fault and the reason why. When the divorce was almost ready to take place, I felt very sad and I thought my mom and dad were kidding and they would not get the divorce. I also felt kind of depressed. When the divorce was taking place and my mom was in court, I felt very, very sad.

Brian age 10

When my parents got a divorce it hurt bad. I thought I was going to die. I took the blame on myself. That was what made me mad. It was like my family was falling apart. I knew what was going to happen to our family, so I tried to stop it.

I thought it was just a bad dream. I thought I was just going to wake up and it would all be over. It's not like that. You have to get over it. But you can't get over it too quick or later in life you will feel it again.

Before you get over the divorce you have to understand it. That means you have to know how the divorce happened. So ask your mom or dad why they got a divorce. If they don't want to answer, ask later.

Chris Age 11

I felt upset, mad, sad, and like I could kill my parents. I feel like I could cry or do something.

One day in the summer, my parents called. It was one week till school started. I came in and sat on the sofa, then my parents started talking. First my mom said that they were going to get separated, then my dad said, "Peter, you're going to live with me over at your grandparents'." All at once I started crying. I felt sad, mad, upset, lonely, confused, frustrated. I thought, *how could my parents do this to me?*

Peter

Age 10

I felt like crying a lot, and I did. I felt very bad, lonely, and confused. I was six years old. I felt sad. It was lonely.

Ned

Age 7

I think it is hard because at first you don't know if you are going to ever see both parents again. It's like you live with one parent and you don't see the other ever again. And you have to have many changes done after your parents separate, but as the years go by it gets easier to understand. I felt sad when my parents had the divorce because I want to have more time with both parents.

Ben

Age 9

My brothers and I felt angry 'cause my daddy threw things and my daddy left 'cause he did not love my mommy. When my daddy was getting ready to leave, he started crying. I did not know daddies cried 'cause I was only four years old. I was surprised Mommy did not cry. A couple weeks later my mommy said, "I really know what I'm doing kids." I like it better now 'cause my daddy does not

Emily

Age 7

throw things. Now my daddy visits me every two weeks which I think is not working out very well 'cause my mommy yells a lot.

I felt like it was my fault, like my parents didn't see me and they were fighting about who would take me. Then I understood. Now it's okay, but my dad has an attitude and it's hard to put up with it, but I do.

Scott Age 10

Before Dad left, my mom and dad always fought. Very often my dad would get mad at Mom for no reason. He would also get mad at me. This was when I was five, so I don't know why Dad was mad. So time went by and I was six when Dad and Mom got divorced. I was sad. But I was six when I knew I should be happy. It sounds strange, but it is really simple. Since my dad was gone there was no more madness or sadness. I was seven when I started to visit my dad for weekends. My dad started to call me. But I was still seven when Dad was going to pick me up, and my dad punched my mom and I could not do anything. By the time I turned eight, and I pretty much forgot about the divorce, but I still could remember a little bit of it. Now I am ten, but age makes no difference. I have about ten friends, but none of them makes up for my dad. I just try to ignore the thought. The beginning is tough, but the end is okay.

David Age 10

When my parents first separated, I felt very sad. As time went on, I felt better. I realized that my mom and dad weren't going to get back together and I tried to accept that. I know now that I haven't

Robert Age 9

really lost my dad. I think I have a better relationship with my dad now.

I've met a lot of kids through Fresh Start for Kids
that have gone through the same things I've gone
through, and that really helped me to know I wasn't
the only one.

I felt sad because I wouldn't have a dad to
play with, and when my mom wasn't home, my dad
could have helped me with my homework.

I felt happy because my dad fought a lot, and a
few times my dad hurt my mom.

I was angry when my dad broke the fish tank and
the fish tank had a lot of fish in it.

I was afraid when my dad hurt my mom.

Tom
Age 10

It really hurts when parents separate or
divorce. That hurt will never leave you. It really is
sad when parents do things like yell and scream,
because it just makes the kids cry more.

Having separated or divorced parents may change
your whole life. That is really sad, because just when
your life was happier than ever, it all turned sad.
The worst part is having to listen to them blaming
things on each other and having to listen to them
take some things out on their kids.

It takes a long time for kids and parents to get
over it. They need this time to sort out their problems. The younger you are the harder it is, because
little kids don't know what is going on. The only
thing you can do is hope that your parents don't get
divorced.

Angela
age 10

Sad. It feels sad and lonely because Daddy went away.

Covington
age 6

I don't like it. It feels really sad to me because I really want to see them both and I don't want to just see daddy on one weekend and not on another weekend. I'd like to see Daddy every weekend and Mommy during the week—that sounds fair to me.

Anders
age 8

I felt sad.

Jason
Age 10

I don't remember because I was only two and a half. I want my mom and dad to be together.

Grace
Age 9

My parents got divorced when I was very young. I was sad and unhappy when my mom left my dad and me.

Vicki
Age 8

Some of my friends' parents are not separated or divorced. But my parents are separated and are going to be divorced very soon. It makes me feel sad.

Lynn
Age 8

I feel sad that my mom and dad are separated. I don't have two prayers at night; I just have one prayer at night. I feel scared at night.

Joseph
Age 9

It feels sad because I was not used to not having both parents there with me. I felt nervous going to a new school. I did not know anyone. It was strange going to a Catholic school.

Jason
age 11

It feels sad because when your parents get divorced you feel very unhappy inside. You should not interfere with the divorce, and it's not your fault.

Billy
age 10

I feel sad when I see my friends with their dads. I wish I could have a dad living with me, because their dads play with them and help them with their homework. My dad lives in Maryland now. I see my dad once a month.

 Even though my dad can't help me with my homework, my sisters help me. This is okay with me.

Becky
Age 9

It feels very depressing, but in some ways it is good. My dad was cheating on my mom. Not any of us were happy about the divorce, except that we didn't have to put up with staying up all night waiting for him.

Siddum
Age 12

Sad. I felt sad because I don't get to see my daddy very much. I would feel better if he lived in the same house.

LINDSEY
5

When my dad first said he was going to live with his friend, I thought it was something I did.

I was scared because my dad was leaving. I didn't know what to do until one day I was talking to my aunt and she said the separation wasn't because of me. I was happy it wasn't what I did. It was because my parents weren't happy together. I remember when my mom would cry because she was in a lot of pain. I felt so bad for her because she had to go through this just like I did.

Hannah
age 10

I don't feel as bad anymore because it's been one year since my parents were divorced. So God helped me get through it. He didn't let it ruin my life. I still miss my dad. I love my parents very much. But when I go to my dad's, I miss my mom. When I'm here with Mom, I miss my dad, so I call every once in a while. Sometimes he takes my brother and me out to dinner, so that gives me a chance to see him and be happy.

I can't really remember what the divorce of my parents was like. I was two or three when it happened. There were sad and angry feelings in my dad and my mom. They fought and argued. It made me a little sad. My mom moved after the divorce. At first I wondered where my mom was. When I got older I was sad and angry. I thought it was my fault. I kept thinking that they would get back together again.

Debbie
Age 14

After a period of time I learned that it wasn't my fault and they wouldn't get back together. Today I'm still a little sad and angry.

It felt like I had no friends anymore, that I had no family. I thought the whole world was against me, even my mom and dad. I also felt that I was no good

Joe
Age 14

and that it was all my fault. It was hard to stop feeling this 'cause I had the lowest self-esteem in the world.

Well, it feels upsetting. It feels good
and bad. I feel upset because if I leave, one parent will miss me. If I go with the other parent, then the other one will miss me. I feel good because I can sleep and don't hear any more yelling, and I don't have a headache all the time. I feel bad 'cause I think I am the problem, but I'm not really. In school I used to get bad grades, like Cs. I used to try really hard, but I always got worried about my mom, dad, Doug, and Brian.

Dana
Age 9

When my parents divorced, I felt
like crying a lot. I was very sad and mad about my father leaving. I thought that it was all my fault and that maybe if I would have been a better or nicer kid, they wouldn't have gotten a divorce. But after a while and now that I've grown a bit, I realize that it wasn't my fault.

I know now how foolish my mother and father were to split up. My father remarried, and so I can never have a real family again. I can never feel that bond between us. I think that it is a very bad idea for parents to separate or divorce because the kids always get stuck in the middle. You may say, "Oh, well it only involves the parents in the divorce," but that is usually a false statement. Most of the time the kid feels sad, mad, and it can even become a painful experience for them to go through.

Daryl
Age 11

I was six years old when my dad left. It didn't make me feel any different because my dad was always away. I remember the day my dad left.

It was a Sunday. We were all going to church, but my dad decided to stay home. When we got home from church my mom realized that my dad's car was not there, and she knew immediately where he went. She went to his apartment and was crying hard. I didn't know what was going on until my mom told me that Dad had left.

I felt sad and glad at the same time. I was sad because I had never been without a dad before. I was glad because there would be no more fighting between them.

Carrie
Age 12

I was sad and unhappy. I didn't like that we were getting a divorce. Daddy had to leave me. Daddy and Mommy fought over me. Mommy wanted me. Daddy wanted me. I didn't like to see them fighting over me.

Katie
age 6

When my parents first told me they were getting a separation, I felt lost and confused. I thought, *Oh, no. What's going to happen to me now?* I was scared. I mean, I thought, *Where am I going to live and with who? Will I move away from my friends and family? Is there anyone the same as me?*

My friends and family tried to help me as much as possible. The divorce brought me closer to my mother. I talk to her more now than ever. It hurts a lot, but not all the time. I am glad I had friends and family to help me then and now. My father lives about an hour and a half away. He still comes to visit me a lot.

Shawna
Age 12

I felt kind of sad!

Marisa
age 6

When kids find out that their parents are getting a divorce or they are separating, the feeling that some children get is very hard to cope with. When my parents got divorced, I didn't really know what it meant, but when other people told me what it was, I was extremely upset. Even though I was able to see my dad every weekend, it was still hard to cope with. I suddenly realized later in my life that what my parents did was the right thing to do.

The overwhelming feeling of guilt was unbearable. At first I didn't think that it was my fault, but as I got older I started to think that it was. It was so hard for me to deal with, so my mom started me in a school program. The program was on telling the kids of divorce that it *isn't* their fault. After going through two years of this program, I started to realize that it wasn't my fault. My parents were just too young. But if I hadn't gone to that program, I probably would still think that it was my fault.

Tanya
Age 14

It took me many years to grasp the fact that my mom and dad were never going to get remarried. For the longest time I wanted a real family with no stepparents or stepbrothers and sisters. I wanted my real parents and a baby sister. My parents were divorced when I was six and now I'm fourteen. I still dream of having a real family and having a nice house, all living as one big happy family. But, now I realize, eight years later, that I can't have a real mom and dad that are married.

For kids of divorce, they go through so much. They need help, just like I did. It's hard on the parents, too, but from some of the things that I've been through, we probably have the worst experiences and feelings to go through. We need a shoulder to cry on, someone to lean on and to be there for us when we go through a separation or divorce of our parents. We need a helping hand to guide us.

Chapter 2

My New Life

I don't get to see my dad every day. I see him every other weekend. We just moved into our home last year, and now we are going to have to move again. Next month we are moving to our grandmother's house. I will be close to my school. I will miss the house we live in now because it is bigger, but my grandmother has a big dog.

Travis age 13

We just moved into a new house and now we are going to have to move again to my grandmother's. I can't go ice skating on Friday nights because I have to go visit with my dad. I'm not looking forward to moving. I will miss my best friend who lives next door. I like my grandmother's dog, so that will be good. Before I could stay home with my dad when my mom went out, but now I have to go with her because I can't stay home alone.

Lauren age 10

You don't get to spend as much time with your parents. We were living in South America before my parents divorced. We had to move to the

Karla age 7

35

United States, which was a big adjustment. I miss the way my dad looked and the things he did with us.

We have to live in an apartment now, so I don't see my dad as much. Not having a house or a yard to play in has been hard. We lived with my grandmother for a while. She has a house.

Josh
9

My dad doesn't live with us anymore. My relatives have different feelings about my dad than I do, and that is hard to hear. My dad lives out of state and I only see him once a month. My mom didn't work before the divorce, but now she works full-time. There is pressure sometimes not to talk about my mom's boyfriend or my dad's girlfriend with the other parent. The other thing that has changed is that my brother goes away to boarding school. I don't know if it is because of the divorce or because of his grades in school.

Carrie
age 15

Dinnertime has changed. It is usually rushed because now my mom works and can't make dinner until she comes home. My mom picks us up from school to save time. I only see my dad once a month because he lives in another state. He couldn't come home for my birthday and that was a little disappointing.

Mandy
age 8

We had to move about an hour away. My dad was a pastor and he had to leave his job. I went to a different school, and fortunately made new friends.

John
age 11

After the divorce, we had to move from North Carolina to Georgia. We had lived in Georgia originally, so the move back wasn't too bad. It was good to have a support system in place with close friends who I could talk to and who knew the whole situation.

Mandi
age 15

The biggest thing that has changed is that my family has gotten a lot bigger since the divorce. Both of my parents have remarried, and that means that I now have a new mom, a new dad, new grandparents, a new brother, a new sister, new uncles, and new aunts.

Kelly
age 11

My dad left. My mom had to get a full-time job. I had to become more independent. Moving was a big change. We moved from Chicago to North Carolina. We moved in with some friends, and it was hard because sometimes I felt like they didn't want us there. It was hard to leave our church back in Chicago.

Amanda
age 13

My dad usually wasn't home before the divorce, so after the divorce I didn't really miss him. The change came in going to visit him every other weekend.

Chris
age 9

My mom got remarried when I was seven years old and my dad got remarried when I was eight years old. My relationship with my dad wasn't as strong as I would have liked it to be. I only

Becky
age 11

saw him every other weekend. After the divorce, we moved from Ohio to Pennsylvania to live with my grandmother. Later, we moved again when my mom got remarried.

My family life didn't really change because my parents and I never did anything as a family. What did change was that my mom and I had to move to my grandmother's house. I fought with my uncle and grandfather. I did not like living there at all.

Anne
age 16

One thing that was frustrating was that my parents never fought in front of us, so we never knew there were any problems. My dad told us that they had a fight and that my mom was going to spend the night at our aunt's house. One night turned into a week. I moved in with my mom after that because I missed her. Then we moved to a different place. Then we moved back home when my dad moved out of the house. Our house is for sale now, and the sign is like a billboard that my parents are splitting up.

Toni
Age 14

We have to go through so much to coordinate our visitation with our dad. Scheduling conflicts and arguments about visitation are very hard. My dad got married about a month after the divorce which was a major adjustment for me. Before the separation, if I had a question to ask my dad I would just go downstairs and ask him. Now it takes so much effort to get a hold of him to talk to him. The availability of my dad has been a hard thing to lose.

Jessica
Age 15

I feel like I have a different life than I did before my parents split up. Everything is different. At first, I lived with my dad for about two years because my mom moved out. Then my mom got custody of us and she got remarried, so I now live with her, my stepdad, and my stepbrothers.

Lauren
age 13

The whole family changed and everybody's attitude changed. We were angry at God at first for allowing this to happen to us. Now things are better for all of us. I was the first one to go back to live with my mom. I wanted to live with her and be her strength.

Jennifer
Age 17

What changed is that I don't see my dad as much. I visit him every other weekend. The fighting has decreased since my dad moved out. They still argue a little bit when they talk on the phone or when my dad comes over to pick me up for visitation.

David
age 9

On Saturday mornings my mom would come get me from my dad, and I was very sad to leave him at home by himself. I would go and visit with my mom and grandparents, then my mom would take me back to Dad on Saturday night. My dad and I would sit on the back porch and watch my mom drive away. We cried sometimes. We tried to hold our sad feelings back and would start playing together.

Zack
Age 9

I was two years old when they separated. I would pray almost every night when I went to bed for Mom to come back home. This went on for three and a half years. My dad and I started going to a church where I learn lots about Jesus and His love for us. The people really helped as much as they could, but they could not help us fully because there were only families that were together and were never separated or divorced. My dad then found another church that helps us in ways we thought that did not exist and in ways we could understand. Church of the Saviour has a program called Fresh Start for Kids which helped me explain and deal with my feelings.

I have to go back and forth to my mom's place and to my dad's. I get to see a lot of different places, like the zoo, parks, and I meet new friends to play with. I received more toys to play with, because I had two Christmases. I saw more of my dad's parents, because we ate supper there a lot because Dad didn't know how to cook very well. We ate a lot of TV dinners. During the day I stayed in a day-care center that I hated. The best part of the day was when my dad came to pick me up.

My brothers and I always fight. My mommy and daddy do not try to like each other.

Emily
Age 7

When my parents divorced, my dad and mom had to move to different houses from each other. That means different schools, different telephone numbers, and most of all different friends—you lose some and get some. My dad's brother John did not want my mom coming over anymore because she was not a part of his family anymore. At first I did not

Brian
age 10

like the school I was going to go to. Everybody was picking on me just because I was smaller.

One new thing is houses. My family and I moved from a big house to a very small house. But our family is still the same. My dad also moved from a big house to a tiny house. Another change is my dad moving away. I was so sad.

Chris Age 11

I have to live at my grandparents' house and get less care and attention. I have to use the phone to get in touch with Mom and the guys.

Peter Age 10

Now my brother Peter and my dad live at my grandparents' house. We have a different schedule. We have to use the phone to get in touch with Dad and Peter. I also now have two birthdays, two Christmases, two Easters, and so on.

Ned Age 7

I have to move to a new house and a new school. I have two Christmases, two Easters, two birthdays, two New Year's Days.

Ben Age 9

I was very lucky because I didn't have a whole lot of things that changed. The biggest change was that my dad had to move to an apartment. My mom has to work every day and doesn't have as much time to play with me.

Robert Age 9

I don't have a dad anymore. My mom and I moved to a different place. We moved to an apartment. We didn't have all the furniture we used to have. We moved from New Jersey to Pennsylvania. I met new friends. I didn't start school in New Jersey. I started school in Pennsylvania. I started a whole new life without a dad. I don't visit my dad anymore.

Tom
Age 10

A lot of things change when your parents get divorced. I think the hardest thing is not being able to see your parent as much as you would like to. I am glad I am not like some other kids, because they don't get to see their parent at all.

Another thing that changes is you don't have two people to turn to and talk about things you need to talk about.

A big change for me was that my mom had to work extra hard to get money to pay for the house. I usually don't get to see her that much each night because she has to work overtime a lot. There are really a lot of changes.

angela
age 10

I don't see Daddy all the time. We moved from our house and had to go someplace else. Mommy had to get a job so we could have some money. Mommy doesn't get to spend much time with us anymore.

Covington
age 6

I had a little brother. My dad got married again, and they live in New Jersey. Daddy doesn't live with me and I miss him sometimes, and I want to see my little tiny brother—he's a fun little dude.

Anders
age 8

We moved from Virginia to Pennsylvania. I had to make new friends. We did not have a car. My mom works. We live with Mom's parents. I don't have a dad where I live with Mom.

Jason
Age 10

There was only one person (my dad) taking care of me. I never saw my mother again after the divorce. Not even my father knows where my mother lives.

My dad had many girlfriends. One girl was named Mary, and I liked her because she gave me gum and invited me to her house. Then my dad met Robin, and I liked her very much.

Vicki
Age 8

My mom talks too much! My brother and I have more chores. I'm in second grade. My mom works full-time.

Lynn
Age 8

My dad moved out of the house. My sister and I have more chores. My mom has to go to work. When we get home, my mom isn't home. She gets home at 5:00. My dad moved into Reading, Pennsylvania. My mom has started dating. My dad has been seeing Judy.

Joseph
Age 9

The thing that changed was that I did not go to a public school. I had to go to a Catholic school. I moved to a new school district. I left all my friends. I had to live with my dad.

Jason
age 11

My mom moved and my dad moved. I changed schools for half a year. My mom and dad were divorced. Money was a problem, and so was fighting, yelling, and changing friends. If my mom remarries I might have to do a lot of traveling because if her boyfriend lives in Texas you have to travel from Texas to Pennsylvania, and it's a lot of money for the parents.

Billy
age 10

One thing that changed in my house is that my dad moved away to Maryland. My whole family started crying, even me, when he moved. I was so scared because I thought that I would never see him again. When he left, he didn't even finish the house. I mean that he didn't finish putting on the doors; my grandfather did it. I was only three years old, and I'm nine now. I was too young to remember. And other things are different now, too. We have less money.

Becky
Age 9

The main thing that changed was that I didn't have a dad and that we weren't having to wait up for him to come home. Then there was that we didn't have enough money and food.

Siroun
Age 12

I used to be happy. Now I am sad. I just want one room to live in instead of two rooms.

Lindsey
5

The first couple of weeks after my dad left, I didn't get to see him that much. I wasn't used to not

having my dad come home and giving us a hug.
After a while I got used to it.

So now I live in a different house and I go to a
new school. I have new friends, a new room, new
block, etc. I got used to it after a while.

My mom started seeing new people. My dad was
living with a lady (who I don't know if she's a Christian). But if my dad gets married, I'd have a lot of
stepbrothers, sisters, a stepmother, and grandparents. And if my mom gets remarried, I'd have an
even bigger stepfamily.

I like both of the people my parents are seeing
because they love me and I love them. It's just that I
wonder why my parents ever got married if they
couldn't get along. I wish there was no such thing as
divorce. I'm also upset about my parents loving
different people than each other. But I guess I can't
change the fact.

Hannah
age 10

There are only a couple of things that I
know of that changed. One thing that changed is
that there aren't as many bitter feelings. If my
parents stayed together, everyone would be miserable. Another thing that changed is that my brother,
my father, and I depend on each other heavily.

Debbie
age 14

One thing that changed is that both
my parents live in different places, but I'm only able
to live with one and visit the other on weekends.
Another thing that changed was who would get
which house and what car.

Joe
Age 14.

Well, there's only one parent, and maybe Mom or Dad won't let you have friends over unless you keep your room straight.

*Dana
Age 9*

The things that changed when my parents were separated and divorced were their personalities. My mom didn't love my dad anymore, and my dad didn't love my mom anymore. We had to live on only one person supporting the family.

*Carrie
Age 12*

Not that much changed when my parents got separated. My father moved out. I lived with my mother. My dad took some of the furniture.

Some things did change, I mean some for the best and others for the worst. Most for the worst. The best was that my parents are happy. My dad isn't there to play softball and other sports. He took a couch and a TV plus the computer. My life was not changed as much as other people's. That I am happy about. No matter how you look at life, things will change, hopefully for the better. We just have to adjust.

*Shawna
Age 12*

Dad lives someplace else. It is hard leaving my mommy and stepdad to visit my dad. And it is hard leaving my dad and stepmom to go to my mom's house.

*Katie
age 6*

Some of the things that changed for me were not being able to live in the same house with my mom and dad. Another big thing that changed was the fact that I was only able to see my dad once a week.

For younger kids of divorce (ages 6-10), changes are hard to go through. They need help. It was hard for me because I wasn't able to see my dad as often as I would have liked to. For older kids, it could be hard or easy. If someone who was my age found out that their parents are getting a divorce, it could be very hard on them if they love both parents very much. If their mom or dad was moving somewhere far away, and they were only able to see that parent once a year, it could be very hard. If it is hard for them to deal with, they might resort to doing something drastic, such as running away or even killing themselves, if worst comes to worst.

A case where it might be easy for them to deal with it is one where they don't like one of their parents and that parent is moving away and they don't have to deal with him/her.

Changes can be fast or slow, hard or easy. Fast and easy are what most kids I think would prefer. I certainly would. But not all divorces can be that simple, meaning that some parents fight over who gets custody, and they fight over visitation rights. I know someone who has it good. She gets to see her mom and dad. One week her dad takes her; the next week her mom has her. Both parents live in the same neighborhood.

Other kids only get to see one of their parents. That can be very hard on the child if she/he loves the other parent very much.

There are many things that change in divorce. It's very hard on the parents and the kids. There are certain things that parents and kids can do or places they can go if they are having trouble going through difficult changes.

Tanya
Age 14

Things change when your parents get

divorced or separated. Like maybe your parents don't
have enough money. You will be changing schools,
changing friends, and changing your surroundings.
Maybe you're better off without a parent. They may
have abused you or hurt you. Some people can change
and some people can't. They may have a problem.
Nobody is perfect.

Danny,
Age 10

Chapter 3

My New Family

My mom has a boyfriend and my dad has a girlfriend.

My mom's boyfriend is nice and we do things together. He is going to help me rebuild a minibike that I found in the woods. We went golfing and he let me drive the golf cart. He takes us to church and then we go out to breakfast. I don't feel bad that my mom's boyfriend takes the place of my dad at times because I like him.

My dad's girlfriend lives in Boston so I don't see her as often. I like her, too, and she is nice.

I don't want my parents to get back together again because they are already split up, and I like my mom's boyfriend. It wouldn't bother me if my mom got remarried or if my dad got remarried. My relationship with my dad has gotten better since my parents separated. We do more things together now. We went tubing down the Brandywine River. We go to the movies and go miniature golfing. I miss the freedom to ask my dad for money whenever I need it, and I miss him coming home for dinner every night.

My relationship with my mom has changed a little bit. She has to take me to the mall and do other things that my dad would do. My mom has to

Travis
age 13

51

work, and that has been a bit of an adjustment for me. She gets tired more and we have extra chores.

Both of my parents have new friends now.

My mom's boyfriend has kids who are nine and twelve years old. They visit us the weekend that I'm not at my dad's house. They go to church with us. Sometimes they go out to dinner with us during the week. Sometimes I fight with them over toys. My dad's girlfriend is nice too. I wouldn't mind if either of my parents got married again.

Lauren age 10

My relationship with my dad has changed because we do more things together. We go bowling, go to the park and play catch, or go miniature golfing.

If I could talk to my dad right now, I would

ask him to come back to live with us. Then we could live in a big house instead of an apartment.

Karla age 7

My relationship with my dad would be

better if he still lived with us because he could play soccer with me. He could also take me on trips and visit different countries. My mom doesn't have as much time to spend with me because she has to work and then come home and cook dinner for us.

Josh 9

I'm closer to both of my parents now

because they are not together anymore. We spend more individual time together. Now I have to be friends with each of their dating partners. I like them

Carrie age 15

both and don't feel like my mom's boyfriend is going to take the place of my dad. My dad doesn't have just one girlfriend, but I have liked all of them. One day my mom's boyfriend was at home with us and then my dad and his girlfriend came over and they met. That was very uncomfortable. My dad writes me every week and he calls me almost every day. I miss my dad coaching my soccer team. I did wish that my parents would get back together, but now that they are dating other people I have given up on that idea.

I don't really talk to my dad unless he calls me. My mom is very rushed now that my parents are divorced. I like my mom's boyfriend. My dad's girlfriend gets mad at us sometimes because when my dad comes back to visit us, she wants to spend time with him, too. I think she is jealous of us. Sometimes I wish my parents would get back together again, but I guess I wouldn't mind if my mom got married to someone else, unless it would change things. It would be hard to share my parents with someone else.

Mandy
age 8

My relationship with my dad has changed for the better. He spends a lot more time with us now. He is nicer now and shoots baskets with me and takes us out for pizza. My relationship with my mom has gotten worse. She doesn't spend that much time with us. I don't really care if my mom gets married again. When we visit with her we swim and watch videos.

John
age 11

My dad has a girlfriend but I have never met her. If they get married, she will never be my stepmom. She'll just be my dad's wife because she was one of the reasons that my parents got divorced. At first I didn't want my mom to get married because I felt like she would reject me and leave me, too, if she found somebody else, but now I am looking forward to her dating because I want somebody to replace my dad. I want this new person to like me along with my mom, instead of just being my stepdad because he is married to my mom. My mom and I were always real close, but we have gotten even closer since the divorce. I can always talk to her and tell her how I am feeling, and I know she will always be there to listen to me.

Mandi
age 15

My mom got remarried when I was three years old and my dad got remarried when I was eight years old. I was in my dad's wedding and that was pretty neat. At first I was jealous of my stepmother and my stepsister. When I found out that my dad and stepmom were going to have a baby, I was afraid that my dad would love the new baby more than he loved me. (It seems like I have more time now with my dad since the divorce.) When I'm with my mom, we don't go to Sunday school during the summer because she is Catholic. I like going to Sunday school in the summer, and that is something I miss.

Kelly
age 11

I don't have a very good relationship with my stepmother. She goes to a Catholic church every Saturday just to look good. My dad worked with her when he was married to my mom. My dad and step-

Amanda
age 13

mother have a baby girl now. I have a stepbrother, but I don't see him that often. I don't see my dad very much and he doesn't call me either. I only tell him things that are really important to me. We are a little more distant now because we live in two different states and he has a new family. I depend more on my mom because she is my only parent now. My mom works a lot so I have to take on more responsibilities. It would be nice if my mom got remarried, but it is up to her. It doesn't really matter to me. I am probably closer to my brother and sister because of the divorce.

My dad had a girlfriend and she was pretty nice. My mom had one boyfriend, but he wasn't very nice. I wouldn't mind if either of my parents got remarried. My mom and I have gotten a little closer since the divorce because we are together more. My dad isn't mad anymore when we visit him and that part is good.

Chris age 9

My mom took a lot of things out on me when she was upset about the divorce, and that was a very hard time in my life. Now we are close and things are better. I have a stepbrother and two half sisters. My dad has been married three times and has three daughters from three different wives. My stepmom is strict, but she is nice and we get along pretty good. At first, I was mad that my dad was getting married to my stepmom because I liked a different girlfriend he had dated before my stepmom, but after I met my stepmom, I really liked her and thought it was all right for them to get married. I

Becky age 11

don't think he will get divorced again, because they
get along. My stepdad is pretty nice. He hasn't taken
the place of my father and we get along pretty well. I
was jealous of him at first because he was taking my
mom away from me because they were always together.

Both of my parents have gotten remarried.
My dad left my mom because he wanted to marry my
stepmom. He was living with her about a month after
he moved out of our house. The adjustment to all
these new people in my life was hard. When my mom
told me that she was getting remarried, I went out
and ate this gigantic ice-cream sundae because I was
so depressed.

I didn't like my stepdad at first. He has four other
children from four previous marriages. I don't get
along with my stepdad's daughter either. I think she
feels like I have taken her dad away from her. I guess I
feel like I have lost my mom because she doesn't do
anything with me anymore. We were very close after
the divorce, almost like best friends. Now that she is
remarried, we have gone back to being mother and
daughter. I guess her emotional needs are met now by
my stepfather instead of me.

*Anne
age 16*

I was close to my dad before the divorce, but we
have since drifted apart. He wants to be with my
stepmom more and not really worry about me. I don't
get along with my stepmom's daughter. Maybe it is for
the same reason I don't get along with my other
stepsister.

Sometimes divorce makes it seem like everybody
has new parents, and that can cause jealousy among
the children involved. Sometimes the parent you live

with might say bad things about the person who is now married to the ex-spouse and their children to create jealousy also. It gets very, very complicated when parents divorce and remarry and you have stepfamilies and half siblings. It gets all jumbled up. Maybe this is why they call these families "blended families." To me it feels more like a "milk-shake family," or if you eat at Dairy Queen maybe a "blizzard family." You put in all the different ingredients, a parent or two, a couple of kids who may or may not share one or both parents, and after you mix it all together you get a "blended family."

It was hard getting used to new relationships with my dad's girlfriend and my mom's boyfriend. I visit my dad every other weekend. I like the girl he is dating now. My mom's boyfriend is a friend of the family. His wife died when my parents got separated, and then he and my mom started dating. At first it was strange seeing them together, because I used to see him with his wife. I've gotten used to him dating my mom now though.

Toni
Age 14

At first I got along very well with my stepmom. I think we were both trying hard to like each other. Now we don't really talk that much. We get along, but we don't have a genuine relationship. I'm jealous that my dad spends more time with her when I'm visiting than he spends with me. When I'm visiting, I feel like he's ignoring me, and he acts like my stepmother is more important than I am. This hurts me because he hardly ever sees me and then when he does see me, he doesn't want to spend any

Jessica
Age 15

time with me. My dad and I get into lots of arguments because he wants custody of my sisters, and I don't think he should have custody of them.

At first I didn't want to believe it, so I was really mad at my dad. But now I am closer with my dad than before. I've gotten close to my mom also because we talk more. My dad is dating a girl now who was a friend of my mom's. That is kind of strange. When my mom first started dating my stepdad I was still living with my dad. At the time, my older sister was living with my mom, so she got to do lots of things with my mom and my stepdad. I was jealous and felt left out of everything. It seemed like they were always having fun and we were forgotten. I like my stepdad now that I live with him and my mom. I get along with him just fine. My stepdad has two sons and they live with us too. That was another relational adjustment that I had to make. I get along with one of them, but not the other.

Lauren age 13

The effects of the divorce didn't hit me hard until my four other siblings came back to live with my mom and me about a year later. I felt rejected by them because when I was living with my mom, they still had to live with my dad. I had to deal with my parents' divorce as well as the separation from my brothers and sisters and how that affected them. At first my mom and I didn't get along because I was jealous of my stepdad. Now things are better.

Jennifer Age 17

I have grown up a lot faster than someone who didn't go through this experience. My dad and I were talking to each other but didn't get along for about a

year and a half after the divorce. Then we went to a
Christian concert and listened to what they were
saying about relationships. We realized we were both
being childish and that we are important to each
other. I realized then that time is short and you have
to love each other before it's too late. We are fine
now and he is the best thing in my life. He is always
there to encourage me to fulfill my dreams and goals
in life. Because I drive now, I spend time with both
of my parents during the week.

It was hard getting used to my stepdad. When we
go to my grandparents' house, it used to be my mom
and dad together, and now it is my mom and
stepdad. This has been an adjustment for my grandparents to make as well. My mom's new marriage is
still new for me, and I'm still not sure if I like it too
much. I don't get along with the stepbrother who is
my age. My younger stepbrother came to me one day
and wanted to know how to have a personal relationship with Jesus. I told him and we prayed together. I
believe now that the reason my mom and stepdad got
married was for me to lead my stepbrother to the Lord.

My dad has gotten married again. I like
my stepmom. I knew her before my parents got
divorced. I've gotten to know my stepmom's parents
and brothers and sisters. They are all nice. My dad
buys me stuff now because he misses me. I feel like I
have gotten a little bit closer to my mom since the
divorce.

*David
age 9*

I have a stepmom who is a very, very good
person. I help her do things in the kitchen and help

her do the laundry. I have many new friends who have stepparents, too. I have new cousins, aunts, and uncles, and we spend a lot of time together at birthday parties. I have a new set of friends from my mom's boyfriend. It's really a lot of fun to have so many people who care about me.

Zack Age 9

When my mom found my dad, she had
seven brothers and sisters. My mom married my dad, so now my mom has about eight brothers and about still one sister. My mom had my brother first, then I was born. I really love my brother, except sometimes it feels like I hate him, but inside I really love him very much just like I love my mom and dad very, very much. I have really met a lot of people since my mom and dad got the divorce.

Brian age 10

When my mom started dating, I hated
when she paid more attention to her dates than to me. But now I know my mom loves me very much.

Your mom loves you very much also. Ask her if you don't believe me. Even if she is going out with her boyfriend, she still loves you very much.

Chris Age 11

It wasn't hard for me to accept new rela-
tionships in my parents' lives. My parents haven't gotten remarried yet, so I don't know what that will be like, but it might be fun to have some new kids in the house.

Robert Age 9

My mom has had two relationships since she divorced my dad. When my mom was dating a guy I felt okay because I might have had a dad. I want a stepdad that likes kids and loves the Lord.

Tom
Age 10

I don't really know what it would feel like to have a new family relationship because I don't have one.

All I know is if I had new people in my family it would really be hard to get used to it. The reason why it would be so hard is I wouldn't know if I could trust them and I wouldn't know how they would treat me. For example, if the person had kids I don't know if they would treat me nice or not. It wouldn't be the same either because they wouldn't be my real family.

Angela
age 10

Daddy got married again, and I have a new little brother.

Covington
age 6

I like Ingrid. She is a nice person and she is funny. Ingrid is my daddy's new wife. She is my stepmom. I like it because either way I get to see two moms who are really nice.

Anders
age 8

My mom dated. Mom goes out with friends and I never see her. My dad is married again. I have a half brother. My half brother gets more attention.

Jason
age 10

I have a stepmother, half brother, and stepgrandmother. My half brother makes me jealous because he gets all the attention. Sometimes my stepmother is mean. She doesn't kiss me good night.

Grace
Age 9

My mother has had many new boyfriends who are rich. My mother didn't let me meet them.

Lynn
Age 8

I prayed to God to give me a new mom. It took a long time, but now I have a new mom. She is nice and beautiful. God is my hero.

God gave us all a baby boy. His name is Blakely. I don't think of Blake as my half brother. I think of him as my whole brother. He is so cute, and I love being a big sister. I love my whole family!

Vicki
Age 8

My mom is on the phone with boys. My mom has started dating. My dad has Judy coming over.

Joseph
Age 9

My dad married a new person. She is nice and she helps me do some of my schoolwork. She helps me with projects. And she is a good cook.

Jason
age 11

I have a new stepmother. They are going to get married in September. To have a fair share of the kids, one parent gets the kids for six months, the other parent gets the kids for the other six months.

Billy
age 10

I now have a stepmother with three step-brothers and sisters. They are very nice.

Siroun
Age 12

When my dad left we all started crying. My mom knew that my dad was going out with a lady. My dad got married May of 1990, and we were in the wedding. I almost started crying. Now I have a stepsister, and she's younger than me. My brother lives with my dad, and he is older than my stepsister. I love my dad very much and I want a dad in my family. It would be *very* nice.

Becky
Age 9

Mommy and Daddy do not love me as much. They do not get to play with me as much. I love Mommy more than ever, and more than Daddy.

LINDSEY
5

If my mom gets remarried I would have a big stepfamily. If my dad gets remarried, I would probably have just as big of a stepfamily, I guess. The new people I've met I really like. I think they like me. It's really nice that I can meet them and stuff, but I don't like to know that maybe they might be a stepparent or something step to me because that means my parents are getting married to someone else. That's not a great thing to know because you already have a dad or have a mom. To know they weren't able to work things out isn't the best thing to know. If they get remarried, then you have more people to work things out with. What if the remarriage doesn't work out? That would make things worse for the parents and us the kids.

Hannah
age 10

I love my parents very much, but if they can't love each other the way God loves us, it doesn't make you feel real good inside. If there is a new marriage, I hope it does work.

Both my dad and my mom have relationships. My dad is going out with a woman named Robin. She has one son named Robbie. They both come over a lot. My dad formed an attachment with Robin, and my brother with Robbie. I want her to be my stepmom. I never really had a mom. My mom is dating a man named Bruce. She has been dating him for a few months.

Debbie
Age 14

I feel good about Dad's girlfriend. And I feel good about my mom's boyfriend.

Marisa
age 6

New relationships were hard because of who my parents dated. My mom is dating someone who I really don't get along with, but I like the lady who my dad dates. Both parents date two entirely different people. The lady my dad dates is kind and sensitive and has a good sense of humor. But the guy my mom dates can be a real insensitive person who only thinks about himself and uses his humor to hurt other people, even if he thinks he's just joking.

Joe
Age 14

I have a new daddy, and a half brother Michael, and Rocky. I have a new mommy.

Katie
age 6

New family relationships aren't

easy to adjust to. Actually, they're quite hard to get used to. My mom has not had many relationships since my dad. She has been seeing someone for a year and a half now. At first it was okay, but then it got worse, much worse. The worst part was his daughter, Sarah. She's eight years old. The first night that they stayed at our house, she went through my things. It gradually got so bad that I had to go to a counseling agency and get help.

Tanya
Age 14

When I found out that my mom got me into a counseling program, I was so mad. After I went to the counselor, everyone around me was starting to see changes in me, for the better. I was getting along with Sarah much better.

The parent who the child is living with should expect some problems. If the child/children have problems, try to work it out. But if that doesn't work, my advice is for the parents and the kid/kids to go to a counseling session.

Listen to the child/children. Listen to what they are having trouble with. Try to help as much as you can, and if that doesn't work, get help. They might not appreciate it if you send them to counseling at first, but in the long run, it's probably, in most cases, the best thing to do.

It takes time to get used to seeing a total stranger come into the house and be around a lot. If the child is used to getting all of the attention and someone else comes into play, some of the spotlight is taken away, and the kids feels as if all of it is being taken away. It hurts to see that parent spending a lot of time with that other person. That is one of the main reasons I had to go into counseling. I needed help realizing that someone else needs some of the attention.

All the kid needs is someone to be there if he/she needs someone to talk to.

Chapter 4

Where Is God?

I feel like God has been near us during this time. It helps when I pray. I pray that we will have enough money to pay the mortgage. God comforts us, and He helped me with my anger towards my parents' separation. If I didn't have a relationship with God, this whole thing would have been more difficult. I wouldn't have anybody to pray to. Last Christmas, we prayed and someone in the church gave us presents.

Travis age 13

God has helped us through this experience. He has been near to me. He helps us out a lot. He helps my mom. I pray and He comforts me when I'm sad.

Lauren age 10

God helps to comfort us when we are sad.

Karla age 7

God is mostly with you, helping you get through your parents' divorce. God was near to me.

Josh 9

God helps me feel comfortable in my situation—living in a single-parent family.

God is always there when you need Him
and need to talk to Him. I asked God why my parents got divorced. God has been close to me and has comforted me. God helps me control my anger. I prayed more for my parents than myself because of the pain they were going through.

Carrie

age 15

God has helped me because He watched
over me. It would have been hard if God was not there. I prayed that God would get my parents back together again.

Mandy

age 8

God is right in the middle of my heart and
has helped me get through this. He guides me and is always there in the bad times and the good times. I pray for my mom to stop smoking and to come back to the Lord.

John

age 11

God was right there with me, even though
at first it took a lot for me to realize that. Without Him I couldn't have made it. My youth group has been a support for me, and my youth director would always be there to listen to me, even though at times he couldn't give a response. He was there to let me talk about it when nobody else was around. At first I prayed that God would bring my dad back home to live with us. Now I pray that God will bring him back

Mandi

age 15

to the center of His will since he has gone so far away from God. For my mom I prayed for strength and that she would be able to get through it.

God is in my heart. He is behind me with every step that I take. He tells me what the good and bad choices are, and He helps me in the hard times when I feel really down. God has helped me when I have been upset to let my feelings out instead of keeping them in.

Kelly age 11

With God's help I am able to tell my dad how I feel about the divorce. I had always dreamed of getting my parents back together again, but now I pray that they can at least be friends. I pray that they can talk to each other and work things out and not get into fights. God has helped me realize that you have to take this step by step and live with the reality that your parents will never get back together again.

God has played a big part in all of this because I know I can talk to Him all the time about anything. It feels like I don't have an earthly father, but I know I have a heavenly Father who cares for me. I pray that my dad will come to know God. I pray for my mom being a single parent with three children, that she will have strength and that God will help her.

Amanda age 13

God has just helped me through it. I prayed that I would forget about the divorce and just go on with my life.

Chris age 9

God has helped me get along better with
my stepparents and get on with my life. I prayed that I
could get along better with my stepdad and that I
would have a better relationship with my father.

Becky
age 11

He helps you deal with the divorce and
gives you the strength you need to get through it.
When I read the Bible, it calms me down when I am
angry or cheers me up when I am depressed. I pray
that my parents will stay healthy. God has helped heal
the hurt and made me realize that it wasn't my fault.

Anne
age 16

After my parents split up, I started going
to my church youth group. God has helped me
because whenever I ask Him to be there, He is.
Sometimes I have trouble asking for His help. I asked
God to let me help other people who have similar
problems.

Toni
Age 14

For a long time I was as far away from God
as I could be, but it was my fault and not His. My
behavior was not pleasing to God. Thinking back on
that experience, I think that it was my way of rebelling
against my parents, and it was a response to how I felt
about their separation. When one of my best friends
had to go to a rehabilitation center for addictions, it
made me reevaluate my own life. I thought about
where I was with God, and I realized that I was hurting myself, too. I stopped doing those things and gave
my life over to Jesus. My life has changed for the
better since then because God has helped me turn my
life around.

Jessica
Age 15

God is in the middle and helps pull you through it all. God is always there for you. I prayed that the whole thing was a dream. When I opened my eyes and realized that it was real, God was there to help me deal with it.

*Lauren
age 13*

For me, God was right there all the time. Whenever I feel down I read the poem, "Footprints," and realize that the reason there is only one set of footprints in the sand when I am down is because God is carrying me through those hard times. God is so good. He has comforted me when I have pain in my life. The Christian music I listen to is also comforting. Wayne Watson's song, "Friend of a Wounded Heart," has ministered to me, because every time I listen to it I see Jesus with love in His eyes and His arms open wide. I know He is there for me every step of the way. I don't know what I would have done without God's help.

*Jennifer
Age 17*

God is up in heaven. He helps you when your parents get divorced. I prayed that I would be okay. God is close to people when they are sad about things. God helped take away the sadness in my life.

*David
age 9*

He has helped me stop being really angry and has taught me to be thankful that one of my parents is not dead. He has taught me to pray, to be helpful to others, to control my feelings, to forgive, to trust Him more, to know it is not my fault.

*Zack
Age 9*

During the divorce I was very sad, mad, upset, worried, and confused. Sometimes I thought that God was sleeping or watching TV or something, but not listening to me. I was going through a hard time. God helped me through the divorce very much. God is very helpful.

Brian age 10

When my mom and dad got divorced, I thought God forgot me. But He never forgets anyone. Sometimes I wish God was all mine. If you think God doesn't love you, you're wrong. God always loves you.

Chris Age 11

He is there to comfort me, help me, make me feel better. He is in my soul to heal me.

Peter Age 10

He is here to heal me and to comfort me. When I talk to Him, He listens.

Ned Age 7

He is in my soul to heal me, to comfort me.

Ben Age 9

At first I was mad at God and I didn't pray for a long time. Then I realized it wasn't God's fault and that I needed God to help me get through the divorce.

Robert Age 9

God was with me the whole time to heal me and strengthen me. God was watching out for us even when my mom wasn't looking for Him. God made sure all our needs were met during my parents' divorce.

Tom Age 10

I think God was with me in this problem because I got through it the best way I could, and I couldn't have done it without Him.

He helped us through our problems. I know that because now my parents are really good friends and there is no more fighting. They worked everything out together, and we really couldn't have done it without Him. He helped us a lot.

Angela age 10

God is watching us in heaven and He's kind of sad.

Covington age 6

I don't really know. If my dad and mom were together I probably would be a little happier. God is probably watching over Dad, Ingrid, Eric (my baby brother), Covington, me, and Mommy.

Anders age 8

He's with me. When I'm hurting He comforts me with new friends, Marvin (my cat), Bible verses, and songs.

Jason Age 10

God comforts me with songs about Him when I go to church, and when I share my things with others.

Grace Age 9

God was with me when my mom and dad got a divorce, and I felt better when I heard that. He provided our needs.

Vicki Age 8

God is in my heart. God is in heaven. I hate Satan! God is right beside me helping me to deal with the divorce. I love God!

Lynn
Age 8

In our hearts with us. He is in our hearts helping us with our problems. He is in our dreams.

Joseph
Age 9

It felt like God was not with me or my parents. It seemed like God just did not matter when that happened. But if God was not there, it would have been a lot harder.

Jason
age 11

It felt like God wasn't there when they got divorced. I was scared and frightened. I thought God didn't care about me. I thought my mom and dad would never see each other again. But I was wrong. God was there for me all along.

Becky
Age 9

God is right next to me every single time I need Him there. He always tells me to come up to Him and snuggle up to Him.

Siroun
Age 12

At first I forgot about God. My dad said he was going to live somewhere else. I was shocked. I didn't really think about God. I thought more about my pain and the hurt I was going through. After a while I saw how much pain my mom was going through. Even though I forgot about God, He didn't forget about me. He helped me get through the divorce.

Hannah
age 10

I was a little mad at God because He let my
parents get divorced. My parents got divorced
because of their unhappiness. I was mad at my mom
because she filed for divorce. I hated that because
my dad would not live with us anymore or be
married to my mom anymore.

Thank goodness God was there the whole time,
because I would never have gotten through the
divorce without His help. I was glad God was able to
help me. He helped me by giving me good friends.

I think God is in heaven and all around us.
He protects us, cares for us, and loves us.

Billy
age 10

God is in every member of our family's
hearts. He is helping to heal the wounds. He gives
us hope and is helping everyone get on with their
lives. He helps to get the divorce over fast. God
helped my dad make important decisions.

Debbie
age 14

God is in heaven. He still loves Mommy
and Daddy and Lindsey even when they are separated. God still cares.

LINDSEY
5

God's with you, but it doesn't always
seem like it. When you're down, He picks you up.
When your parents or even my parents divorced, I
thought it was God's fault a little because He let my
parents get divorced. But it wasn't His fault. He was
there along the way to pick up my whole family, and
He showed me that it wasn't my fault. It was really

Joe
Age 14

no one's fault. It's just one of those things that would have happened anyway. I would have liked to stop it, but I couldn't.

God is always with you when parents separate or divorce. I know God was there for me. He made my mom overcome the separation and divorce.

Carrie
Age 12

Personally, I think God is right there with you. I mean, from experience, the things that God does, He usually does for a reason. My dad, who is not proud of it, has been divorced three or four times. But look at him now. I mean, now he has a dog named Lindy, and he is happily married to Lisa. My mom has remarried a wonderful guy named Bob, and I now have a baby brother named Adrian who is two years old. And my mom is now expecting another baby girl whose name is Jesse.

Elliot
Age 12

Some people think that when their parents divorce or separate, that God has left their life because they did something wrong and He will never come back. When my parents divorced, I was angry at God, and I thought I had done something wrong. But after about a month, I realized that God had not left and that I hadn't done anything wrong. That made me feel happy, but I was still very sad about the divorce.

When my parents divorced, I would pray to God to ask Him to get my parents back together. After they divorced, like I said before, I was angry at God. But He was right there with me. He helped me understand why my parents got divorced. He also helped my dad find a guy named Gary.

Gary was the one, along with God, who helped me understand the problem. That is where I think God is when your parents separate or divorce.

He is in your heart trying to make you happy!

Marisa
age 6

In my heart trying to help me a lot. He tried to cut off bad parts and bring in the good parts. God helps me pray.

Katie
age 6

Chapter 5

My Story

I was four years old when my dad stopped living at home. It is too far to think back, so I don't remember what it was like when my parents were living together. I remember I felt both happy and sad. I felt sad because I thought I would never see my dad again. I felt happy because there was no more yelling at home. I did get to see my dad for a while every Saturday. That made me happy, but I was sad because I would miss my mom. I am not spending time with my dad now. When I did visit, he would buy me candy and toys. I liked riding in my dad's truck.

Jesse
Age 6

When my dad moved out, we got a dog named Ginger. My mom started to drive me, my sister, and my brother to more places, like the playground, so we could ride our bikes. We would go swimming in the indoor pool during the winter and the outdoor pools in the summer. I like the indoor pool better because it has a diving board and is warmer than the outdoor pools. We also started going out to baseball games and the library with my mom. We get to go to Utah to ski with my aunt. That is my favorite thing to do.

I spend a lot of time with my grandmom now,

because my mom is always at college. When both my mom and grandmom are gone, I get to play with my granddad. I wish my mom could spend more time with me. I just had the chicken pox, and my mom had to leave me alone in the bathtub to take care of my sister and brother. That made me mad and sad. I wanted her to stay with me. I like it when she reads only to me at night, and then we cuddle.

I learned about God in Sunday school and at home. Jesus lives with us and helps me. He heals my hurts.

My mom and dad got divorced when I was just a little baby. I was glad I was too small to hear about the divorce. But when I got a little older and realized my parents were divorced, I was very sad when I heard it. My heart was broken.

When I was five years old, I went on a train trip to see my dad. (He lives in South America and was here in America for business.) When we saw him we were very happy, because it had been four years since my mom and dad got divorced. I didn't know anything about him because I was so small when the divorce happened. I liked getting to know my dad a little bit. It was very painful to see him leave after the weekend was over. We were having so much fun.

Karla age 7

I feel better about the divorce now, because it's all over with. I might be able to see my dad again, but for now I'm fine. I'm happy to live with my mom because she takes good care of me, just as my dad would. Fresh Start for Kids helped me to know I am okay because other kids' parents are divorced, and I know it's not my fault.

Sometimes my mom and dad
would argue. I was happy till the separation. I always felt loved.

Jeana
Age 7

Who was going to take care of me was my most difficult worry. The second worry was who was going to move out and who I was going to be with the most.

It helped to pray to God and to talk to Mrs. Huffman, the counselor at school. I talk to Beth Hanna and Courtney and Mrs. Huffman, too. They help! I like to talk to my best friend Shannon.

Life was perfect before everything
happened. I remember in kindergarten when I'd come home early and my dad would come home from work and eat lunch with me and my mom. Before everything happened I didn't have to pack a bag to see my dad. Life was great. Everything was too perfect. I sure do wish it was like that now.

Mandy
age 8

The hardest part was to go to school and have to tell people about it. And it was odd not to have a dad here. Nobody else in my class had parents who are divorced. Every time I thought of it I couldn't believe it had happened.

What helped most was my psychologist, and what helped some was just not thinking about it.

It hurts sometimes to think about the
separation. After six months you lose the pain. But then maybe one of your lost parents will come back and give you the pain again.

Luke
Age 8

I was sad when my parents stopped living

together. I was only six years old and just beginning
the first grade when my parents first separated. The
best feeling I had was being relieved that Dad moved
out, because I didn't like all that fighting and stuff. I
also remember feeling scared when I would come
home from school to find Mom and Dad yelling at
each other from the opposite ends of the room. I
would run to my room, close my door, and hide under
the covers. I don't remember what they were fighting
about. I only remember that my dad moved out and
did not live with us anymore. I felt very lonely when
my dad left. I missed the super-hero stories he would
tell me in bed before I would go to sleep.

Chad
age 8

A lot of things changed when my parents separated. My father was not around anymore. Then we
got a puppy, named Ginger, from my Aunt Margee.
That was fun. I like having a dog. I began to do a lot of
sports like baseball, skiing, soccer, swimming, and
tennis, because my dad wasn't around anymore. When
he lived with us, he never wanted us to leave the
house when he was around. Skiing is my favorite
sport. I even get to fly to Utah once a year to ski with
my Aunt Margee and her boyfriend, Gary.

After my dad moved out, I got to ride in his pickup
truck more than I ever did before. Sometimes he even
let my younger brother, Jesse, and me ride in the back
of the truck. We liked doing that. Even though my
parents don't live together, the yelling did continue
whenever my parents saw each other. That made me
sad.

My mom is always going to her university and is
working or studying, so I don't spend much time with
her. That means she can't spend as much time talking
to me as I wish she could. I spend more time now with

my grandmom (we call her T-mom) and granddad, because we live with them and my mom all year 'round. Now I am friends with other children whose parents are divorced.

I always thought God was with me during the divorce. I learned that God will never leave me, and He will do what's best for me and comfort me. I learned that from Mom and Fresh Start for Kids at church.

Divorce is when your mom and dad get separated and live in different places. This happens when they stop loving each other. Divorce hurts. My stomach hurts because I kept my feelings inside. I thought I was going to burst.

Stephen Age 8

I thought the divorce was my fault because I heard my parents arguing about me. It made me feel sad.

I felt like I was being pulled apart. I did not like switching my toys between Mom's and Dad's houses. I felt angry that this was happening to me. But I knew if I wanted to see my parents I would have to live in two different places. Sometimes I forgot my homework at one of the houses.

I thought I was the only one going through this. But later I found out that others went through divorce too. Mr. Hayes helped me the most, because he had a divorce group for kids. We learned how to talk about our feelings and that divorce is not our fault.

My brother helped too. I told him it was my fault and asked him how I could stop the divorce. He told me it was not my fault and there was no way I could stop Mom and Dad from getting a divorce. It made me happy to learn it was not my fault.

It is not so bad now. I get to live in two homes and have twice as many friends. I still get to do a lot of fun things with my parents. Mom will always be Mom. Dad will always be Dad. Mom and Dad are friends now, but I still feel sad sometimes that we will never be a whole family again.

I would like to tell other kids that it will be tough, but you will get through it. If your parents get divorced it is not your fault. Do not keep your feelings inside. Go talk to the guidance counselor, Mom, Dad, brother, and sister.

When my parents weren't divorced I was just fine. I didn't even know what divorce meant. Life was fun before they got divorced.

We had a family meeting when I found out that they were getting divorced. I was very, very sad.

Now I feel okay because I know that my parents still love me, and I get to see my dad a lot. Fresh Start for Kids has helped me a lot because I know I'm not different.

David age 9

It was hard for me before my parents split up. They were always fighting when they were together, but sometimes they were nice to each other. My father was the mean one and my mother was the nice one in most of the cases.

The most difficult thing about my parents deciding to get a divorce was that it came upon me so fast. The night I found out I just went into the bathroom and cried. I felt really awful, and I felt bad because I

Chris age 9

thought that hardly any other kids had divorced parents.

I talked about it with my mother and I asked her why they were getting a divorce. She said, "We still love each other, but we just can't get along." Now I just say to myself, "Okay, that has happened, so go on with your life."

Before my mom and dad got divorced, we had a happy family, especially with a new baby. I don't remember too much about my family then, but I do remember that I spent a lot of time with my dad.

When my mom and dad got divorced, everything changed. We had been living in South America, and then we had to move back to the United States and move in with my grandmother. My mother had to get a job, and my sister and I had to go to the baby-sitter's a lot. It was hard. I also had to stop seeing my dad since he was so far away.

At first I didn't know why they got divorced because I was only three years old. But after a while, I got over it with God's help. Right now I am nine years old, and I don't really think about my mom and dad's divorce. I understand now that it wasn't my fault, and right now we have a happy family—my mom, my sister, and me.

Josh
9

We had a normal house before the divorce, just my mom and dad always fought. The time of the divorce, Dad took me and my sister with him so we didn't feel like Dad didn't love us anymore. He brought Mom's best dominoes so my sister and I

Lindsey
age 9

could play with them. That was the day of the divorce.

Now I have to go back and forth between houses. Talking to the people at Fresh Start for Kids told me that I'm not the only one going through it.

When I was nine, my parents got divorced.

The first time they told me about it I didn't know what was going on. It was like I was in a bubble and I couldn't get out. One day I even went to my brother and said, "Pinch me." He did and it hurt.

Kristin
age 10

My parents always argued when my

dad got home. My mom would start crying and my dad would walk away or else leave the house. I listened in my room and cried. Right away I knew something bad was going to happen. Sometimes I was mad, but I think I was mostly scared. I had mixed feelings about my mom and dad.

Lauren
age 10

One day I was out with my dad. He told me that he and my mom were getting separated for a while. I cried the whole way home. The day he moved out, my family and I cried and cried. Now that he is gone my mom got a job. She earns more money for us to live. Sometimes when I think about it I start to cry. I realized things don't always work out how you want them to. My friends try to help me out a little bit. My teacher often offers to talk to me. I'm sure things will work out okay. So far they have.

When your parents get divorced, you

obviously feel sad. You will think that it is your fault, but it isn't. Maybe you think that you were too pushy or too greedy, but it is not your fault. Your parents separate or divorce because the love isn't there. They both love you very much, and they probably will go to court for your custody. The parents will be very sad and sometimes cry.

Sometimes parents will buy you all the stuff you want, but others cannot. Usually your father will spoil you because he has a job. But your mother will too. It's a constant war that no one can stop. Even one of your parents' friends will try to win you over to your dad or your mom. You can make a choice, and you're *not* alone. Almost the whole entire population is a single family or a mixed family.

Danny,
Age 10

You probably have a lot of questions before you want to make a decision. Maybe you don't and you already know who you want to live with. For the kids who don't know and do have questions, I may have some answers. Your first question will maybe be, "Will they stop loving me?" The answer will be no. Because they are not living together doesn't mean that one or both are going to lose interest in you. Your second question may be, "If I didn't do something or did do something, they would be together still." Your answer there is easy. Nothing you did or didn't do made them separate or divorce.

There are too many questions to answer, so I am going to tell you about my family's separation. When I was seven my mom took me to a women's shelter before my dad came home from work. I've been in court about five times a year. I miss school a lot of days because of this, and I miss having a whole family. Today I live with my dad. I like it.

What is this world coming to! We don't know.

When my parents got divorced, I was
only five. I was very sad. I started going back and forth
between them. This is my schedule: one weekend at
Dad's house and one weekend at Mom's house.

Susannah
Age 10

I'm the third youngest of five. When my
parents got separated, I was three years old. Then my
parents got back together for two weeks, then they got
divorced. I don't remember it because I was young. He
would come to our house for dinner some nights, but
they would fight.

Melissa
age 10

Divorce. A word I never knew. One day I
heard the word divorce. I went to look it up in a
dictionary. It said, "To end a marriage with."
I said to myself, "Mom and Dad aren't going to be
married anymore."

So I asked my mom why she and Daddy were not
going to be married anymore. My mom said, "Dad has
found someone else to love."

Because of my father's choice, we had to move to
Melmark. It's been hard, but with God's guidance and
strength, we will make it.

Jeffrey
Age 11

It's weird at first. You don't think it will
happen. Then it does. Your parents aren't together.
Soon it really affects you. You have to travel to get to
your other parent instead of just walking a few yards.
But it's not your fault! You are not alone. You don't
lose a parent. It's like getting two small presents
instead of one big present.

Danny
Age 11

We had a pretty normal life, but my mom
and dad always seemed to fight. When the day of the
separation came, I was four. They were crying and I
wondered what was going on. That night Dad left
and got an apartment. The first night there we got to
sleep with Daddy so we didn't feel like, "Oh, Dad left.
He doesn't love us anymore." So that was the day of
the divorce. I have to go back and forth between the
houses. Being able to talk to someone about it made
me know that I wasn't the only one who went
through this situation.

Lauren
age 12

All my aunts and uncles were there. My
Aunt Betsy gave me a quick hug and ran to my
mom. "You look beautiful!" she said. "I think you
picked the right one." She was talking about a
wedding dress, of course.

Becky
age 11

It was a few days before my birthday, and I was
about to go down the aisle as a flower girl. No one
had even said happy birthday.

The day before my birthday, someone finally
wished me a happy birthday. I was beginning to feel
jealous of my stepfather, but that soon changed. I
had a special birthday that year because my mother
could see how I felt.

After my birthday we moved. It was strange living
with someone who wasn't my father. I felt almost
protective toward my real father.

My stepfather tried to be nice, but I felt he was
trying to take my dad's place. I was angry at both of
them.

I have a stepbrother. At first I was excited about
him coming for the summer, but later it seemed like
everything they did was to make him comfortable.

Later his mother remarried and divorced again. That summer they paid almost no attention to me. "He's been through a lot," they said. *I've been through a lot, too!* I thought.

Many times I would go into an angry phase over nothing. I would cry and cry for no reason, and they would yell at me because I could not give an explanation. When I would share my story with other kids in my situation, they would answer with a story twice as bad.

When my parents saw how I felt, they sent me to counselors, and the counselors helped me to talk about my feelings that I didn't want to talk about with my parents.

I can deal with the feelings about my stepbrother and stepfather now. My name is Becky, and I hope I never feel like that again.

When my parents first decided to split

up, I felt very mad at my mom because she left my dad and took us with her. From then on all they did was fight like little children. I was also mad at my dad for having an affair. For me that whole year was pure madness!

A lot of things in my life changed. I have to baby-sit my brother all the time, which is very boring. I can't get all the clothes I want. In addition to that my mother is so nosy. All of a sudden she'll get this distinct feeling that I've been doing something wrong when I haven't. Why can't she be like other mothers?

My relationship with my mom is horrid! On everything, we disagree. We always argue and she's always mad at me for some dumb or stupid reason. She wants my room clean, but I can't find anything

Missy
age 11

when it's clean, but she still wants it clean. I say "tough luck." She yells. I yell. I lose and get busted. That's how horrid it is.

Some new people that have come into my life are my mom's "men friends." Some of them are dumb and some are groovy. Usually my mom has one of her friends come and pick me up from soccer or school.

God has helped me when my parents fight or when my dad and mom fight with me. He carries me when my life is really hard. So thanks a lot, God!

I was really young when my parents got a

divorce. It's been ten years and both are remarried. My mom has two children, one's seven and one's nine. When my dad got remarried, his wife already had a child who was six years old. It's been two years since my dad got remarried, and his wife is having a baby.

Kelly age 11

I lived with my dad for seven years and went to visit my mom every other weekend. I went to day care after school because my father was at work. I found out that my dad was very different from my mom because my mom would let me stay up later than my dad would let me stay up.

I never thought my parents got along very well. I never really wanted my parents to get on the phone or talk. It just did not feel right to me. I could tell my daddy and I were really close, and so were my mom and I. My daddy and I had a different kind of relationship than my mom and I. For example, my mom and I like going shopping and doing things together. My dad and I like to do things like play games, read together, and take walks.

Before my father got remarried, it felt like we

wouldn't be as close. I feel the same way now that my dad's having another baby.

Whenever I see my mom, I feel happy, and we do a lot of things together. She seems to spoil me a lot. I guess it is because she doesn't see me much. My friend lives with her mom, and it seems to me that her mom spoils her more than her dad does.

I'm not glad my parents got a divorce, but now when I think of it, it seems that if they did not get a divorce, they would always be fighting. Now both of my parents are remarried, and I know they will never be together again.

When I was in third and fourth grades, I went to a place called Rainbows, and it helped me understand why my parents got divorced. I learned that it was not my fault. I moved so I could not go to that school anymore. The school I moved to did not have a program for children of divorce. As I grow older, it seems to get harder and harder for me to accept my parents' divorce, and it is confusing for me.

Before Mom and Dad got married they both worked at Donnelley Printing Company. Then Dad met Mom and they got married. They went four years without any children and then I was born. Then four years later my sister was born and six years later Mom left.

John

age 11

At the time my dad was a pastor, and then Dad had to leave the ministry, and I lost a lot of friends and neighbors. I also had to change schools—that was rough. It was hard for both of us.

There are a lot of stages you go through. The first is the worst—sadness. You cry a lot in this stage. The second is when you feel like you were the reason your mom or dad left. Don't think that; it's not your fault. The third is anger. You feel a lot of anger over the person who left, but don't let it get you down.

The fourth stage is when you start to get over the anger, the fault, and the sadness. The fifth stage is when you start to forgive the person who left. I know you don't feel like loving the person, but always love the person who left. The most difficult thing to get over is how or when your parent left. The best thing to do is to go happily with the parent you live with and have a good time. What has helped me the most is having a good time with my dad, who I live with, and with my mom when she picks me up to have a good time.

My mother and father got divorced
when I was four. We had just moved to Michigan. My mom's not married yet, but I'm still happy. My dad and I used to have fun. We acted the same a lot. I don't know what I really felt when my mother and I left my dad. My mom and I went to live with my grandma until I was five. Then we moved to Farmington Hills, Michigan. We lived there for not even three years. We moved to Pennsylvania, and I've lived here for five years.

One day my dad called. He said, "How's school?" He started laughing, and I hadn't even answered yet. He's an alcoholic. I'm happy about living with my mom. He told me in a letter that he was moving to South Carolina with his girlfriend Beverly. I've met her before at my grandmother's house. She has three kids, Steven 24, Wendy 18, and Holly 15. I like Beverly. She's very nice. My dad called another time

Jaime
Age 12

and he asked my mom if I could visit him in South Carolina. I was very scared. I didn't want to go. I just want to stay with my mom.

When parents separate or divorce it hurts. You feel both parents are never going to meet each other again. Also it feels like they're never going to help or talk to each other for the rest of their lives.

Well, this is how it might feel, too, with God. You're with Him for all your life so far. Your parents teach and tell you how to love God, and you know He is here in your heart. But when your parents separate or divorce, it seems like God leaves or takes your heart with Him because your parents are leaving each other and you're sad. And it feels like nobody is living inside you, or nobody is even around you anymore.

All of a sudden you realize God is hoping for the best for your parents and it will turn out fine. God will always be there for you, helping you through every step of the way.

When my parents got divorced I was little, too little to understand why. As I got older I started to understand more and more, and it started to hurt. At times I felt empty, like something was wrong and definitely missing from my life. I wasn't sure what it was though. I often considered believing the idea that I was the cause of it. Then in my mind I liked to play a game and blame my younger brother for the divorce. It made me feel better. But my brother and I were close (nineteen months apart), not only in age but also in the way we spent time together. I really wanted a dad, but not the one I had. He smoked. He drank. And he made what seemed to be wonderful promises which were never fulfilled.

Courtney
Age 13

After I hadn't seen him (my dad) for a long time, I began to forget about him. I was happy with my life. My dad lived in New Mexico and we lived in New Jersey. My mom, my brother, and I were all content with our small little family. My grandparents were great supporters. My mom was working a lot so we had our fair share of baby-sitters.

Everything was fine until my dad wanted to be part of our lives again. I immediately said "no way" because I was afraid of the possibility of him leaving again. Eventually he came to visit. Then he decided to move to New Jersey. My brother and I saw him every weekend. We got very attached to him, my brother more than me. About a year and a half later, Dad moved back to New Mexico. He called for the first few weeks and then just stopped. We were devastated.

Finally, I got mad and wrote him a mean letter stating how mad I was and how I wished he would pay child support. Ever since then he doesn't call me. He calls my brother.

I figured out what the emptiness was—not me, not my brother, and it wasn't my father. It was the relationship I longed for with Jesus that I have now. I know Jesus will never stop loving me or leave me, like my father did.

Maybe someday I will regain my relationship with my dad, but Jesus healed my hurt feelings and my angry ones toward my dad.

Hi, my name is Lauren and I'm thirteen.

My parents have been divorced for three years. I have two sisters, Jennifer and Katie, and two brothers, Jamie and Chris.

I never dreamed my parents would get a divorce. I always thought my parents would be together forever! Of course my mom and dad fought. And of course they had their differences, but doesn't everyone?

My father's a dentist and works in Calhoun, Georgia. My mother's a physical therapist and works in Rome, Georgia. They hardly ever spent time together—even when they were together I don't think their hearts were.

Lauren

age 13

My parents split up for about a month, then got back together. Three years later my two sisters', two brothers', and my life were ruined, or so I thought.

When my parents went to court the first time, my father got custody of all five children. We were all upset. My father and my oldest sister, Jennifer, who was thirteen at the time, fought constantly. The second time Mom and Dad went to court Mom got custody of Jennifer, and they split us up! I didn't think judges did that to kids. How can you split up five children who have known nothing except each other and their two loving parents?

My mother and father went to court a couple more times, and I think the fifth time back the judge asked to see the youngest four children. This time the judge granted my mother full custody of my brothers, my sisters, and myself.

I think that what really got me through this whole ordeal was my faith in the Lord. He definitely watched over me and everyone in my family. Mother's and Father's love, support, and guidance gave me the strength to go on and to be myself.

This year has been a real change in my life. A lot has happened, and a lot is bound to happen in the future. I moved for the first time in twelve years, my mother got married, and my father has started dating.

I'm so much closer to both of my parents now. My father was extremely upset when we left, and he was hard to talk to. Now I can talk freely to both of my parents. I love my father and mother so much. They're both extremely precious to me. They really encourage me to be my own person, to do my best at everything, and to pursue my talents.

My life was really great before my parents split up, but it's great now, too. Life goes on. You might feel as if your life is completely over, but you have to be strong, not only for yourself but also for your parents.

Don't let the pain of divorce mess up your life; give your parents the love they need. It's hard for them, too.

On January 3, 1986, an eight-year-old girl hopped around the kitchen collecting her father's belongings and placing them in boxes. Little did I, the young girl, know that evening what a difference my dad's moving out would make in my life.

Amanda

age 13

Being so young at the time, I hardly understood the term divorce. All I knew was that my dad was moving to a neat apartment in a nearby town. In fact, when he told my family, my younger brother and I wanted to play Monopoly while my older sister and mother cried their eyes out.

I remember very few things from before my parents' divorce, but one specific thing I do recall is my dad reading Winnie the Pooh books to me before my bedtime. I also know that we used to go to the park for a picnic and often traveled to Wisconsin from our home in West Chicago, Illinois.

The most difficult time for me was the year that they got divorced. My parents fought and yelled every night, and my mom usually ended up stressed out every morning. After my dad moved out, he continued to be verbally abusive and had a hard time with child support. My mom had a hard time for many months, especially with finances. She had to find a full-time job, and my brother, sister, and I had a lot of new responsibilities. If it weren't for close friends and prayers, none of us would have made it through this time of trial.

About two years later in 1988 we got news that my mother's father had cancer in his brain. We went down to Pinehurst, North Carolina, to see him. While we were there, my mom went to Raleigh to visit some old friends. She applied for a job while there and got it. Her news reached my grandmother's house an hour before my grandfather died.

Since then our family has seen many changes. First, my dad got married to a woman he worked with. They stayed in Chicago, but we moved to Raleigh. Not long after that my dad's mother died. He came down to North Carolina for her funeral, then informed us that my stepmother was going to have a baby. Emily Joanna was born on June 19, 1989.

It was a big change for all of us, but now I have learned to accept the fact that my dad lives some-where else with another wife and baby girl. It really helped me to know that friends were always there for me and to know why my parents got divorced. But I will always remember that even though my human father has many faults, my heavenly Father will never turn His back on me, no matter what happens.

Hi, my name is Travis! My parents aren't divorced yet, but they are separated. When my mom and dad were living together they fought a lot, but it was usually after I went to bed. We had a family trip to the shore coming up, but my dad said he didn't want to go because he and my mom would just fight the whole time and spoil the vacation for all of us. He said either he would take us or my mom would, so my mom took us. A couple weeks after that he moved out. Now my sister and I go to his house for the weekend every other week. I don't know if it was better before when he lived here or how it is now. When he was here my parents fought. But now that he isn't here we have to sell our house because the mortgage is too high, and sometimes I miss him.

Travis age 13

I know a person who is very kind. His name is Bud. Every Sunday he comes over and takes my mom, my sister, and I to church. After church Bud takes us out to breakfast.

Whenever we need Bud we can call him, and when he is not home we can call him on his car phone. And when my mom is not home he calls to check up on us. When he comes over to our house he usually stops at a store and gets a candy bar for my sister and me. Bud helps me with my homework when I need help. He also helps me with different things that I make.

Two days ago Bud watched my sister and me because my mom was not home. We watched TV for a while, and my sister asked him if we could go to the store, but he said no. Then about two minutes later he said, "Let's go!" So he took us to the store when he did not even want to go.

Before my parents got separated, life
was lively with busy activity. We had family night every Thursday, church activities on Sunday, and tons of family traditions like hanging a new family

ornament on the tree. (One year we hung a smashed matchbox car on our tree representing when my sister had an automobile accident.) Our family was a real family. My older brother John, nineteen, and my older sister Cindy, twenty-four, didn't enjoy sparing their social time to sit at the table for an hour, but in their hearts they enjoyed it.

Toni
Age 14

My parents owned two companies right underneath my house. When we came home from school every day, we would have the luxury of my parents being close by. One of the bad parts was that at any time of the day or night my dad had to be right by the phone. The businesses failed, and so did my parents' twenty-four year marriage.

My brother and sister both moved out and moved five minutes away to live with my mom. For nine months I faced loneliness and frustration; luckily each day got easier. No one had ever seen my parents fight, so I was in complete shock. Fights occurred a lot when we moved, and that never left my mind.

We moved back into my old house after almost losing it, and now I'm starting to fit life together with a lot of help. But wait, life wasn't all fantasyland before we left. I threw terrible tantrums for years. We even made a trip to the hospital once when I talked of suicide and banged my head against the wall. I didn't want to live—truly I didn't with all my heart. Another person inside was coming out and frightening me so much. I now have grown so much and would like to tell everyone else to hang in there—you deserve it!

My home life before my parents' divorce never seemed quite right. There always seemed to be issues too complicated for me to understand. I remember feeling hurt, and many times I would cry myself to sleep.

For me the most difficult thing about the divorce was not having my dad around for little things like tucking me into bed or making me pancakes on Saturday morning. I also miss spending a carefree day with my mom because she works now and has less time to spare. The simple things that I took for granted are what I miss the most. Even when I'm with my parents and we do things together, it still is different than life before the divorce.

During the divorce I was about twelve years old, and I thought (at the time) that nothing affected me and that my parents' divorce was no big deal. I also thought that getting drunk, smoking, and experimenting with drugs were cool and that they wouldn't change me. Unfortunately, they did. Because I was lying a lot to my mother, she didn't know what to believe. It has taken more than a year to rebuild the trust that she had in me before I started lying to her.

Jessica
Age 15

After getting into trouble with my school, my parents, and the law, I realized I could not handle it anymore. I decided that I needed to quit all of these harmful activities. I assumed that after I quit doing drugs and drinking everything would be great for me, but it didn't work that way. I was depending on my own strength to heal my pain, and nothing was there to fill the big void in my life. I decided that I needed to depend on God for everything. I gave my entire life to Jesus, and all of the emptiness that had been in my heart for years was filled.

My parents still have many disagreements on how to raise my brothers and me, and I usually end up in the middle. But now I can deal with my feelings in more constructive ways, especially when I'm building new relationships and healing old ones. Nothing can fill emptiness in one's life unless it is filled with Jesus Christ. I hope you'll talk to the Lord. I guarantee you will see results.

Life couldn't have appeared to be

more perfect. Sure, like every family we had our problems, but everyone always pulled together to work things out. All of my friends were always commenting on how cute my parents were together and how great a family I had, and of course I always agreed. We spent so many great times together— going to the shore for a vacation or just going to a soccer game together. I knew no two people could have loved their children more. Then, like a snow-storm in July, the divorce came out of nowhere. All of the joy turned to pain and all the happiness to hurt. Each of us had to deal with many new feelings. Whether they were feelings of denial, anger, or depression, we all had to try to pull together to cope with this sudden, new life-style.

Carrie

age 15

There wasn't just one part that was hardest about this life-style, but there were a few. For example, learning to deal with being an outsider and thinking that you were the only one with divorced parents. Or having to listen to your mom, the one you look up to, cry day and night, and there wasn't a thing you could do. There was a feeling of helplessness when she'd break down in the car.

Aside from all that, I had to deal with school. I had to tell my friends what happened, and I got sick of having to tell about it, over and over again. Plus, I couldn't seem to concentrate anymore in class. But, believe it or not, in time things got better, but only because I had the support of my family, a great psychologist, and God above. I didn't seem to mind having to pack a bag to see my dad anymore, and I learned through Fresh Start for Kids that I wasn't alone in this divorce thing.

It has been almost two years, and everyone is holding up just fine. However, I'm having to deal with a new crisis: double-dating with my mom!

Hi! My name is Mandi. I am fifteen years old. My parents have been separated for two years and divorced for one of those years.

Before all of this mess started, things were great. My parents took me and my brother to church every Sunday and Wednesday. We always did something. It was either going out to dinner and the movies, or curling up by the fire and watching TV. I couldn't have asked for a better life. My parents hardly ever fought.

Mandi
age 15

When they told me that they were getting divorced, I was truly shocked. I didn't understand why! It happened shortly after we moved to North Carolina. One Friday night they sat us down on the couch and told us. I didn't quite understand what had happened or why. I screamed and cried. I didn't know how to get my emotions out. The hardest thing for me to accept through all of this was that my dad wasn't coming home, and he also wasn't the same guy I once knew!

I was really close to my dad, and I cared about him a whole bunch. I wasn't quite sure why he had changed. To tell you the truth, I was confused about when the changes had taken place. It was like it happened overnight. My dad all of a sudden turned against everything he once told me. I tried very hard to accept him the way he was, but it just wouldn't work out for us. I would have been able to make it if he would have given a little bit toward the relationship.

Without the help of all my friends I wouldn't have made it through. I tried not to tell people too much, but the more I told the better I felt. My youth director was a lot of help for me. He followed me through all my steps and told me when I messed up. I am here to tell you that happened a bunch.

I really don't need to give all these other people credit, though, when the one who helped me through this the most is Jesus Christ. Without Him on my side, I couldn't have made it all the way to where I am today.

I am back on track and doing well now. I am active at school and on the weekends. I stay pretty busy with church also. People don't see me any differently, and I no longer feel funny around families because my mom, my brother, and I make a happy and loving family. Jesus Christ is the only one who could have made that possible.

I hope you will realize that one day all of this will work out for the best. You need to hang in there. God will pull you through if you count on Him.

My parents have been divorced for six years now. Throughout the years I have experienced many emotions. But the emotion I feel now is acceptance. My life before my parents' divorce was like any child's. I was an only child, so I was spoiled by my parents. My parents and I often took trips. We'd take a day or a weekend and go to places like Strasburg,

Anne

age 16

Pennsylvania, or the B & O Railroad Museum. During my parents' marriage, they never fought. They seemed to be the perfect couple. We lived what seemed to be the perfect family life.

But then one day when I was nine years old my parents told me the news. My mother was very straightforward with me. She told me that she and my father were separating and that we were going to live with my grandparents. At first I was confused; I didn't understand what was happening. But as I thought about it, I started to understand it more.

I then thought it was my fault. The emotion I went through was guilt. I thought that I had done something wrong and that I had caused the problems. I remember one night my mother, my aunt, and I went back to my old house to pick up some things of ours. My father was supposed to meet us there, but he didn't. Luckily my mother still had her key. We invited a friend of my mom and dad's to wait with us until my father arrived. About eleven o'clock that night my father came home. My mother and father had a huge fight. I think this was the most difficult thing about the divorce, mostly because my parents never fought before. While they were fighting, it made me feel that I had done something wrong. Because of this incident I knew that their marriage was truly over.

I've had a lot of help in dealing with their divorce. One of the things that has helped me is the program Fresh Start for Kids. This program helped me because I didn't know any kids my age who were going through what I was going through, and in this program I met other kids who were going through it also. I realized that I wasn't the only person in the world going through this.

My life before my parents' divorce was

perfect, or so I thought. They had been separated once before, so I thought a divorce was out of the picture for good. But I was wrong. I never saw the signs, mainly because I didn't want to. Now when I think about it, so many things were leading straight up to it. My dad was gone a lot, but I just told myself it was his job. Whenever he would leave for a trip he would always carry on like he wasn't ever coming back. Many signs I should have seen but didn't want to.

Jennifer
Age 17

The most difficult thing about my parents' decision to get a divorce was what story to believe. Most divorces have two sides—the mom story and the dad story. They each try to get you to believe their stories. I found it easier just not to listen to either side because it made me crazy! After the divorce I didn't really know who to trust or believe anymore. I never got all of the true story, but I got enough to understand things. Some things I don't think I want to know.

Only one thing helped me deal with the reality of my parents' divorce, and that was my wonderful, awesome God! He carried me the whole way through. Whenever things got really bad I would always remember that God is with us always, even unto the end of the age. He also made something good come out of it. I grew so much in my Christian life, and my dad and I patched things up between us.

The hurt will never leave, and sometimes I still cry about it even after two and a half years. But God proves something good can come out of something bad. The wonderful faith I have in God taught me not to worry so much and also not to give up! And for all the teenagers with divorced parents, He will be there for you.

That morning I left my typical American
family, happy and secure in the thought that it
would be intact when I returned.

I didn't return to a happy home, but a broken one
instead.

The fact that my father was gone did not hurt me.
To me he was not there to begin with. All I could feel
was my mother's and brother's pain and suffering.
All I could feel was the brokenness and tension of my
once peaceful and comforting home. I felt as though
my security and stronghold was crushed. There was
nothing to run to and be safe.

The divorce caused my life, plus the lives of
others around me, to take a complete turn. I no
longer wanted to come home. I was tired of the tears
and constant sadness. I had to watch every word I
said and was careful not to mention the word love. I
felt that I had to be the strong one because everyone
else was too busy falling apart. I lived the rest of the
year feeling out of place in my own life. Nothing was
the same and I felt as though my family would never
laugh again.

Many people told me that it would get better, that
the pain would go away. I truly believe that the pain
would still be here if it were not for the new relationship I found with God. My security was gone, but
I was shown a new security, one that would never
fall apart or lose its ground. He opened new relationships through friends and teachers who are cher-
ished to this day. When my parents divorced, God
was in the same place He has always been—right
next to me. Only through the time of the divorce, He
was underneath me holding me up.

Now, as I look back almost three years later, I can
see God's wonderful working in my life. I've learned

Sandra
Age 17

to trust God through every problem, big or small. I've
seen how all things truly do work together for those
who love Him. I've also seen how God picks me up
and carries me through the eye of the storm.

Chapter 6

Letters to God

Dear God,

Thank You for always being there for me when I need You. Thank You for helping me deal with my parents' divorce. Without You I wouldn't have been able to handle it as I did. I can always count on You, and whenever my pain builds up inside me I know I can tell my pain to You and You understand and help. Thank You.

Love,
Jennifer

Dear God,

Thank You for my life. Why did You become God? Why did my parents get divorced?

Love
C

Dear God,

Help the pain of my parents' divorce to not be there anymore.

Love,
Jiel

Dear Lord,

Thank You for comforting me, my mom, and my dad. I love my dad very much.

Love,
Jason

Dear God,

Thank You for Your love and care. Thanks for dying on the cross for me. I thank You for taking my sins away so I can go to heaven. Thank You for blessing me with a good family that loves me even though they are separated. I'm glad that You're in my life.

Laura

Dear God,

How long will it be till all my hurts stop from my parents being gone? Thank You for giving me two good parents, but not for the hurt. Do You think I will go to heaven when I die? I hope we have a fun time moving, and will You help me learn how to like my new school?

Love,
Kelly

Dear God,

I love You, but there are mostly two questions in my life. Not to say You're not doing a good job, but I need to ask You, why do You let people die you love before you get a chance to say good-bye? Why do You let people get married that You know are going to get divorced in the end? All I know is You have a good reason for it and will always have a good purpose for it. Lord, I do want to thank You for a loving family and a dog that I love dearly. I also thank You for sending Your Son for my sins.

Love,
Elise

Dear God,

Thank You for comforting me. You are a good friend. I wish I could meet You, but I have to wait.

Sincerely Yours,
Charles

Dear God,

My dad is mean to me. They, my dad and my stepmom, are always fighting. Now I really feel it is my fault.

Love,
Grace

Dear God,

My parents are divorced. I live with my mother. I learned that it was not my fault. I have a lot of animals. When they die, please take them to heaven so I can see them again after I die.

Love,
Leslie

Dear God,

Thank You for helping me through the divorce. You comforted me and made me feel good. I needed Your help and You gave it to me. I want You to keep on helping me. I need You and I love You.

Dear God,

I miss my mom and I'm sad because I might have to wait a long time to see her again. I wish that I would get along with my dad. Everything is really going wrong with my family and I'm not happy about it. I hope that it gets better.

Love,
Lori

Dear God,

Thank You for helping me get over the divorce and for comforting me.

Dear God,

Thank You for comforting me.

love,
me

You probably know how I feel about this whole thing, so why in the world I am writing this I do not know, but I'll write it anyway. I feel excellent in some ways and in other ways I don't feel so great. One of these is because we didn't get to go canoeing. That was a bad feeling because I won't get a chance to go for a whole school year unless my dad takes me some weekend. A good feeling was yesterday when I got to walk through a swamp and had a mud fight with some friends.

Now about the divorce. When I was three years old I remember my parents fighting. A few weeks later they broke up. When I was four my parents got divorced and Mom sold the house even though she didn't have to. She also had a yard sale that I remember, and she sold a brand-new washer/dryer set that cost about $600 for $50. And she sold a few other things for real low prices. When it was time to move, Mom wouldn't leave and Dad had to pay the mortgage for two months. That is when they said they would sue, so Mom left, and because my counselor wants me to end now I'll tell You the rest later.

Dear God,

You know that I don't care about my parents' divorce. I just want to know if my grandmother is up there.

Your Son,
Chris

Dear God,

This is how I feel: hate, bad, sad, stupid, different, depressed.

Your friend,
Chris

Dear God,

I love You. I pray to You to help me have a good time when I get home, to help me get through life all right, and for me to know You've got Your loving arms around me and You love me dearly like I love You. You're the only one I can trust always. I know You will guide my family and help them to do the right thing. Please help me to forget the past and start a whole new life with Your love.

Love,
Dana

Dear God,

I do not like it when my mom and dad fight. I get scared. Why do they do it?

Julie

Dear God,

Please help Mommy and Dad. Help me to be comforted and comfort other people who need it. I hate it when Mom and Dad fight. I want them to live together again and be happy.

Dear God,

I know that You let my parents get divorced for a good reason; they weren't happy together. I want to thank You for giving my mom strength to go back to school. It will be good for both of us. Thank You also for giving us the strength to move to Maryland from Colorado. It was a good choice. I made lots of friends.

Love,
Shannon

Dear God,

Here is a list of my feelings:
1. Anger from my parents' divorce.
2. Sadness from my parents' divorce and remarriage.
3. Disappointed in my parents.
4. Bitterness toward stepdad.
5. Scared to talk to my real dad because he will scream.
6. Forgiveness to Mom for wanting divorce.
7. I accept the divorce.
8. Bad for my dad because he did not want the divorce.

Thanks,
Charlie

Dear God,

Thank You for loving me and being my friend. I love You. I don't know how I ever could have made it through my parents' divorce without Your comfort. Please use the hurt and pain I've felt to make me beautiful inside. I want to help other people who are going through the same things. God, I pray that You would show me how to feel about my dad. Help me to forgive him and love him. Please help my mom to heal inside and not worry about everything.

I Love You,
Tricia

Dear God,

Thank You for the Bible. I love You.

Dear God,

I love You. Help me through some things.

Dear God,

Thank You for helping me get through divorce. I love You.

Dear God,

Please help my pair of parents.

Love,
Abbie

Dear God,

You have been so good to me. You helped me to pass every year in school. Also, You help me to make new friends everywhere I go and also You answer my prayers. You are also there when I need You, and I thank You for always forgiving me and dying on the cross for me. Thank You.

Love,
Michelle

Dear God,

Thank You for comforting me when my parents got divorced. Why did my mom and dad get divorced? Did my dad really love my mom when they got married? How much did my dad love me? I'm glad You comforted me.

Dear God,

I want to say I am sorry again for my sins and I would also like to say thank You for all the things You have given me and also for taking care of me through my parents' separation and helping my mom, brother, and me to have a closer and more stable relationship.

Love,
Tara

P.S. About my father, please help him be more understanding and caring toward my brother, me, and, most of all, my mom.

Dear Lord,

I know You know everything, so I will keep it short—I love You.

Epilogue—

A father to the fatherless,
a defender of widows,
is God in his holy dwelling.
Psalm 68:5

My Three Dads

It all started when I was five years old; my parents got a divorce! I don't remember feeling sad that my dad was leaving or that my family was breaking up. I don't even remember feeling angry. I don't remember feeling scared that my family was in crisis. I can't remember even crying. You see, my parents did an excellent job of protecting me from the bad feelings that kids feel when their parents get divorced. There was no pain!

What I do remember about the divorce was that I was getting a "new dad," but I knew that he could never replace my real dad. I was going to live with my mom and my new dad, and I would visit my real dad every Sunday at his new apartment. I remember being proud to be the only kid in school that could tell his friends, "I have two dads now!" They would ask me questions like "Who do you like better, your new dad or your real dad?" and "Why is your last name different than your mother's last name?" I think I felt funny not being able to give my friends any good answers to their questions.

I think the thing I regret the most was that I never got the chance to be angry or sad when I was five years old. I never cried over the fact that my parents were breaking up! I know my parents were only doing what they thought was best. They stressed the idea of moving away from the pain of the divorce and moving ahead to the future of bigger and better things so much that they didn't give me a chance to feel pain or any other bad feelings. I was asked to forget the pain before I had a chance to feel it, and that hurt me very much.

When I turned eighteen years old, my real dad got married again, and I thought that maybe having divorced parents wasn't so wonderful. I was going to have to share my dad with someone else now, and this made me feel sad and angry for the first time. Nobody protected me from the pain this time. I questioned why everybody told me when I was five years old that it would be great having two dads. I didn't even want to come home from college for my dad's wedding because there was a big pep rally the same weekend. I remember having to tell my friends that I couldn't go to the rally because my dad was getting remarried.

I later found a third dad who helped me deal with my parents' divorce. It was my heavenly Father—a Dad who gave me the comfort I needed for the pain. He didn't promise to take away the pain (He will do that later when I get to heaven); He just turned my troubles into a hope that would never disappoint me. God helped me by giving me strength when I was weak, by promising to never leave me when I was afraid, by forgiving my sin so I could forgive my parents' sin, and by giving me peace and love through Jesus Christ. Our heavenly Father is the God of all comfort. He comforts us so that we can comfort others when they have troubles. We can comfort them with the same comfort that God gives us.

One of the purposes for writing this book was to give you an opportunity to read about other kids who have gone through similar experiences you have gone through, and to help you find comfort in the fact that you are not alone. Another purpose has been to communicate the message that you matter to God; God wants to be your heavenly Father and adopt you into His family. We hope that your life has been changed by reading this book because you were touched where it hurts.

Though my father and mother
forsake me, the Lord will receive me.
Psalm 27:10

May God be made famous through this book!

Gary A. Sprague, ACSW
Director, Fresh Start for Kids

About the Author

My Parents Got a Divorce is Gary Sprague's first book. It is a natural result of his own experience as he became a child of divorce himself in 1965 and now works with kids who have lost a parent through death, divorce, or separation. Gary has also written two workbooks: *Kids Caught in the Middle: An Interactive Workbook for Children*, and *Kids Caught in the Middle: An Interactive Workbook for Teens*. He is committed to helping others heal from the pain of being a "modern-day orphan."

Presently working for Fresh Start Seminars, Inc., Gary is the director of Fresh Start for Kids. The seminars are for kids ages 7-18 and are sponsored by churches and schools throughout the country. They are conducted by Gary with the help of adult facilitators who have either experienced the divorce of their parents or have experience working with children of divorce. The seminars are designed to help kids see that they are not the only ones whose parents are divorced, and that what they are feeling is a natural response to a very painful experience. In addition to leading seminars throughout the country, Gary also directs programs for single-parent families.

Gary has worked extensively with children and families with special needs, including grief recovery, residential treatment, foster care, adoption, and family counseling. His professional affiliations include the Academy of Certified Social Workers, the North American Association of Christians in Social Work, and the National Association of Single Adult Leaders. Gary received a master's degree in social work from Loyola University of Chicago, and a bachelor's degree in psychology and sociology from Trinity College in Deerfield, Illinois.

When not spending time with a group of kids or other families, Gary loves to spend time with his own. Gary, his wife Lois, their three children, Skylar, Taylor, and Dylan make their home outside of Valley Forge, Pennsylvania.